Mind over Golf

Alan Fine

BBC BOOKS

Published by BBC Books,
a division of BBC Enterprises Limited,
Woodlands, 80 Wood Lane
London W12 0TT

First published 1993
© InsideOut Development Ltd, 1993
The moral right of the author has been asserted
ISBN 0 563 36376 2

Designed by David Robinson
Illustrations by Dave F. Smith

The diagrams on pages 42, 79, 80 and 81 are adapted from
Mihaly Csikszentmihalyi's *BEYOND BOREDOM AND ANXIETY:
The Experience of Play in Work and Games*, 1975, pub. Jossey–Bass Inc.,
San Francisco, all rights reserved. They are used by permission of the
author and the publisher.
The diagram on page 44 is adapted from *MENTAL TOUGHNESS
TRAINING FOR SPORTS: Achieving Athletic Excellence* by James E. Loehr
Ed. D., 1986, pub. Stephen Greene Press, an imprint of Viking Penguin,
a division of Penguin Books USA Inc., and is used with permission of
the author and the publisher.

A BBC video of *Mind Over Golf* (BBCV 4902) will be available from
Spring 1993.

Set in Garamond by Selwood Systems, Midsomer Norton
Printed and bound in Great Britain by Butler & Tanner Ltd, Frome
Colour separation by DOT Gradations Ltd, Chelmsford
Colour Printing by Lawrence Allen Ltd, Weston-super-Mare
Cover printed by Clays Ltd, St Ives plc

CONTENTS

ABOUT THE AUTHOR

Alan Fine qualified as a professional tennis coach with the Lawn Tennis Association of Great Britain in 1975, and has since coached many nationally ranked juniors. His interest in how people learn and perform under pressure has led him to advise athletes from many different sports, particularly golf, as well as business people interested in improving their performance.

Alan Fine has worked with European tour golfers like David Feherty, Colin Montgomerie and Richard Boxall, and in business his clients include managers from companies as diverse as Dupont, Rockwell, IBM and the British Institute of Management.

Alan Fine has previously written *Play to Win: Golf* with David Feherty and is a regular columnist for *Golf World* magazine.

ACKNOWLEDGEMENTS

So many people have helped and continue to help me increase my understanding of performance. But it is right that I give special mention to a few of them:

To my dear wife Penny whose special insight and encouragement never cease to brighten my life.

To BBC Enterprises and Heather Holden-Brown for the opportunity to write about my favourite subject and their patience with my efforts.

To Gary Cullen (ex-PGA European Tour Professional) whose fault it is that I ever became involved in golf – happy fishing Gary!

To all the long suffering golfers I have been lucky enough to work with, many of whom have become good friends, and especially David Feherty, Richard Boxall, David Llewellyn and Phillip Price, who also allowed me to write about our work together.

To Richard Simmons of *Golf World* magazine who has toiled many unsocial hours to help make sense of this.

And, last but not least, to my two children. They are too young to have any idea of how much they teach me about learning – and yes, Timothy, now the book is finished I will be home for supper!

PREFACE

We hear people talk more and more about the importance of the mind in golf. I tend to be one of the biggest culprits; I'm fascinated by the dilemmas the game throws up. Why is it that we fear short putts? Why do some people freeze when they have to play over water? What drives us to make a mess of a relatively simple shot at a crucial stage in a match? And why is it that we are able to hit the ball well on the practice ground, but never play as well as we know that we can in competition?

These phenomena – and there are many others – cannot be explained in purely physical terms. We spend much of our time learning about the theory of swinging a golf club, and yet we lack the self-control to be able to put that knowledge into practice. The point at which we recognise this is usually the point at which we consider learning about mental skills.

As spectators, it is often the mental side of golf that gives us such drama and excitement. The Ryder Cup matches have perhaps proved more than anything else that at the highest level golf is a game of mental control. Even the world's greatest players feel the strain. Some crack under the pressure of intense competition, while others seem to thrive on a challenge and shift up a gear when the heat is on. However, few of us ever perform up to the level of our true potential for more than a brief period of time. We might play the odd good shot, or produce a good round once in a while, but we find it hard to sustain our performance over any given length of time. The game that we play against ourselves is much more difficult than the one which we play against the golf course. We hit great shots some of the time, and it's these that keep us going when our game won't come together.

I'm not a professional golfer, and in this book I will not attempt to teach you the technical or physical skills that are necessary to play the game. They are covered in more than enough detail elsewhere. What I will talk about are some of the things that I have found to be important in learning and performing these skills.

Golf: The ecstasy (above) and the agony (opposite) of the Ryder Cup

Throughout my career I have been increasingly fascinated by how we can make learning more effective and more enjoyable. I was a tennis coach for 15 years, and during that time I became interested in the work of Timothy Gallwey, whose books *The Inner Game of Tennis* and *The Inner Game of Golf* have brought the mental game into prominence. To me, his work opened the door to applying some of the psychological theories I had been studying and led me to many other interesting new approaches.

Over the last five or six years I have been privileged to work with many professionals from the European tour, including David Feherty, Richard Boxall, Colin Montgomerie, Phillip Price and David Llewellyn – golfers who have through their own experiences recognised the importance of developing their mental skills. They have patiently watched me learn – sometimes at their expense, other times at their gain – and this book is based on all these experiences.

This is not an instruction book covering everything you need to know to play golf! It does not tell you how to swing the club. And it does not claim that if you do all of the things contained within its pages you will take ten strokes off your handicap. It does, however, contain some things that have been helpful to many

golfers, both amateur and professional. These things have been helpful in the sense that some of the golfers have found that they enjoy playing the game much more, find it easier and less stressful to learn the skills they need, and most of all, play better.

I believe that the missing link to reaching our true potential is largely to do with improving our mental approach to the game. It is not all there is to being a good golfer, but with good mental skills we have our best chance of playing to our full potential.

GOLF IS A MENTAL GAME

'Competitive golf is played mainly on a five-and-a-half-inch course, the space between your ears.'
Bobby Jones

HOW MUCH OF YOUR GOLF DO YOU THINK IS MENTAL?

When I have posed this question to individuals and groups I have worked with, the usual response is that golf is at least 80 per cent mental. I've never had an estimate lower than 50 per cent.

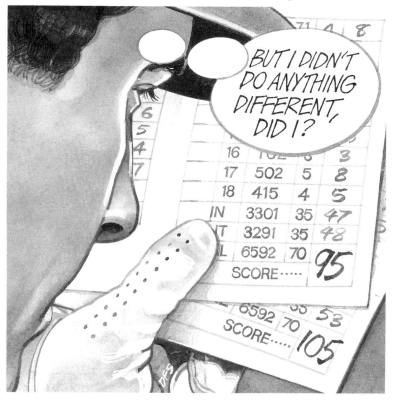

95 one day,
105 the next ...

What intrigues me most about the answers that I receive isn't what the exact percentage is (of course there is no statistical validity to these answers), but that people actually do attribute such importance to the mental side of the game. From their collective experiences, these golfers – both amateurs and professionals alike – are saying that they consider the mental side of the game to be highly important in terms of their overall performance, and at least as important as their swings. I then ask how much of their practice time do they spend deliberately rehearsing and developing their mental skills? And so far I have not met anyone who has said that they devote more than 5 per cent of their total practice time to improving their mental skills.

So let's add it up. On average, less than 5 per cent of our effort is directed towards a part of the game that is generally regarded as contributing at least 50 per cent towards our overall performance on the golf course. Although we may recognise and appreciate the significance of the mental skills, the majority of our practice time is devoted to developing technical skills, i.e. analysing and fine-tuning the swing. As far as I'm concerned, this doesn't add up at all.

GOLF: THE DILEMMAS OF THE MIND

At whatever level we play golf, our performance on the course is determined by what our mind does. Think about it. You can play to your handicap one day, and yet you're 15 over the next; you can hit the ball consistently on the practice ground, but not out on the course when it most counts in competition; you can use all of the clubs in your bag except, say, the 4-iron; you usually play well around your home course, but for some reason always seem to make a mess of the 14th hole; you have no problem with putts of 10 or 15 feet, but become anxious over a relatively simple 3-footer; you can chip perfectly well around the green, but always duff the ball when you're faced with a shot over a bunker ...

'Competitive golf is played ... between your ears.'
Bobby Jones

Despite the wealth of technical knowledge available to us, and our eagerness to analyse and work on our swings, we still wrestle with the frustration of playing reasonably well one day, but terribly the next. While we might go out and shoot 95 on Saturday morning, on Sunday afternoon we can do no better than 105, even though we are playing on the same course, with the same clubs, under the same weather conditions and with the same partner(s).

Whether we like it or not, our performance is determined by our mental state, or as Timothy Gallwey described it in his book

The Inner Game of Golf, the game that is played within the mind – the 'Inner Game'. As the great amateur Bobby Jones implied many years ago, there is a lot to be gained if we can learn to control the workings of our mind when we're out on the golf course, i.e. improve our mental skills.

MENTAL STRENGTH

Watch the top pros on the tour and you will see they all swing in different ways. So what do they have in common? One thing is they all return the clubhead to the ball in a repeatable fashion. While their swings reflect obvious physical differences, they are all remarkably similar at impact – and that's where it counts. And they can all get the ball into the hole in relatively few strokes. Of course, some do this more successfully than others, and it is usually the difference that you cannot see that sorts out the winners from losers. Just as in life generally, the top performers in golf are those players

Ballesteros and Nicklaus – two of golf's toughest competitors who are very strong mentally.

One of the characteristics of a truly successful golfer is that he can still perform reasonably well even when his swing is a little awry. When you hear commentators describing someone as a 'tough competitor', this is usually a reference to that player's ability to keep a score going, even though he's not really striking the ball particularly well. People often describe Faldo, Ballesteros, Langer, Woosnam and Olazabal – currently five of the best golfers in the world – as great examples of players who are mentally 'tough'. Another would be Jack Nicklaus, who in his prime had legendary powers of concentration. When it mattered most he was able to focus only on what he was doing to the extent that he literally blanked out everything else around him.

If you were to follow the scores of the mentally tough competitors throughout the season, you would find that rarely do they shoot scores of more than one or two over par, at worst. These golfers suffer peaks and slumps like everyone else, but they are so

All good golfers return the clubhead to the ball in a repeatable way, e.g. Steven Richardson (left) and Bernhard Langer

Leadbetter on Faldo

I don't think that you can ever separate the mental and physical aspects of golf. They're inextricably linked. The physical exercises that I give Nick are really the tools that he needs for mental preparation. When I'm working on his swing he finds that he is able to relax mentally, and that helps him to absorb more easily the slight changes that we might make. Nick likes to have key swing-thoughts, or feelings, when he plays, and much of the time that we spend together involves developing drills and exercises that keep him mentally focused on what he's doing.

The key word as far as Nick is concerned is 'feelings' rather than thoughts. If you do something that gives you the proper feeling for your swing, you can relate that to what you're actually doing when you're hitting a golf ball. Certainly, if a player is standing over the ball and thinking too hard about his swing in terms of pure theory, he's likely to become tight and tense and lose his feeling for the swing.

David Leadbetter

strong mentally that they are able to survive periods of physical weakness (i.e. days when their swings are slightly off key) on the strength of their belief in themselves and their desire to succeed. As a result, their scoring range is likely to be much tighter than that of the golfer who does not have such capabilities. It seems to be an annual tradition in the Open Championship for an unknown player to lead the field at the end of the first round, and although he might have scored a 65 on the opening day, he usually follows it up with a much higher score on Friday, when the enormity of the occasion hits him squarely between the ears.

At the highest level, it is simply the power of the mind that separates the winners from the losers. During the closing holes of a major championship it is not the leading player's swings that come under the microscope – they have all proved they can play – it is their mental strength and their ability to withstand pressure that is the deciding factor.

IT'S ALL IN THE MIND

Because of the dynamics of golf, the effects of the mental part of the game are more graphic than in most sports. In fact, the effects of anything that you do are magnified greatly, and in that respect golf is much less forgiving toward changes in your mental and physical state than most other sports. The slightest change physically can have a major effect on the outcome, and the precision that's necessary to produce a good shot is phenomenal when you consider the physics involved. The clubhead travels a distance of at least 20 feet during a typical swing, and yet if the clubface is only a fraction of an inch open at the moment of impact, the result is a shot that could be as much as fifty yards off line. Tiny changes in what the club does are indiscernible to us, and so we often cannot tell what it is we are doing differently. Our swings feel the same, and yet they produce consecutive results that are very different.

The unique pace of the game is another factor that contributes to its mental demands. In the four hours or so that we spend on the golf course, only three or four minutes are actually spent swinging the club and executing a shot. The rest of the time we are free to think, to get worried, anxious and generally lose concentration.

In reflex sports, such as tennis, we are much more reactive and our mind is not given the opportunity to indulge in as much self-sabotage. But in golf – a game where we always initiate the action – there is simply too much time to think. We think about our

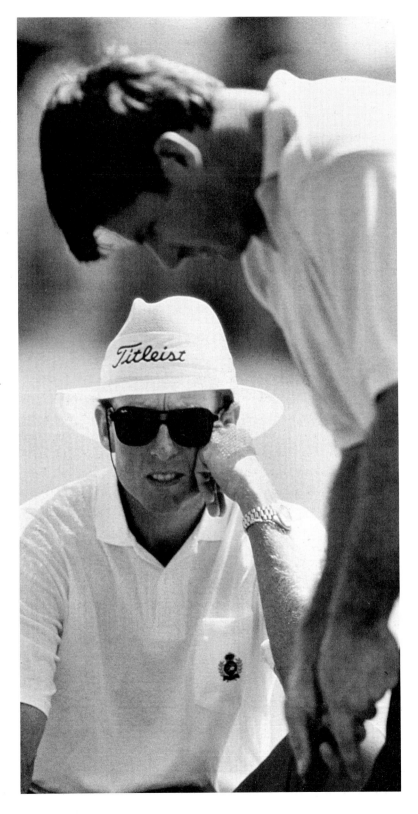

'The mental and physical ... are inextricably linked.'
David Leadbetter

The greatest mind of them all?

Even the greatest of golfers are susceptible to lapses in concentration. The 1981 British Open at Royal St George's was won by the little-known American Bill Rogers, but the early headlines were taken by Jack Nicklaus, who in the first round shot a 13-over par score of 83, his worst performance ever in a major championship. It later transpired that Nicklaus had been told that one of his sons had been taken ill at home in America only minutes before he was due to tee off. That news had naturally unsettled him, but his professional pride stood in the way of making excuses, and to an astonished gathering of pressmen, the man who many regard as the world's greatest ever golfer explained that his 83 was 'the best I could do today – I tried on every single shot'.

It is simply a measure of his phenomenal playing ability – coupled with an incredible desire and absolute belief in himself – that, having satisfied himself of his son's condition, Nicklaus went out the next day and shot a course record of 66.

technique, about what we should and shouldn't be doing; we worry about the trouble that awaits us on the next hole and dwell on the three putts that we just took on the previous one. In other words, our minds are continually busy, and our concentration is therefore adversely affected.

AVOIDING OUR MIND?

THE MIND GAME – THE AREA OF GREATEST GAIN

Looking at the development of sport over the last thirty or forty years, we can see a trend towards technical and physical excellence. Athletes today are fitter than they have ever been before. They use improved training methods, they have the benefit of much-improved analysis and feedback mechanisms, and they eat scientifically devised diets. The net result, not surprisingly, is that our athletes are altogether fitter and stronger and technically more proficient than their predecessors, and their performances are pushing the limits of human endeavour ever further. In fact, they are pushing so hard that we now encounter drug abuse in the sometimes desperate search for higher performance. However, it is the mental skills or psychology that provides us with the area where we can really make the biggest gains because we actually still know so little.

Every physical action that we perform is controlled by the brain. In fact it is impossible to separate the mental and physical aspects of our make-up – we would need a lobotomy to do that – so why then do we tend to neglect such an important aspect of the game?

OUR OBSESSION WITH TECHNIQUE

There has been more written about how to swing a golf club than almost any other human activity. Every month volumes are produced, breaking down the swing into minute parts; there are books and videos meticulously detailing what we need to do to play well. To me, it seems that almost every conceivable movement in the swing has already been described. And it's all sound stuff! But, if all it took to play well was the ability to understand what to do, we would all be in the Ryder Cup team.

Much of our obsession with technique stems from thinking that the more we know, the better we will be able to do it. We frequently work on our swings in the same way that a mechanic would dismantle an engine. We buy videos, read books and magazines and

(opposite) Jack Nicklaus during the first round of the 1961 British Open

21

David Llewellyn 'played like a dog' and scored 68

discuss our swings with other players. We believe that if we hit it perfectly, or like Faldo or Ballesteros, we will play perfectly, and yet there's little evidence of a correlation between the perfect strike and the perfect score, particularly at the top level.

I remember speaking to David Llewellyn during a European tour event. He had shot 76 in his first round and couldn't understand why – 'I struck the ball really well, but all I could do was a 76.' The following day he shot 68 and said 'I didn't deserve it, I played like a dog'. Evidently, being able to reproduce a perfect strike or swing doesn't necessarily equate with being able to produce a perfect score. Ironically, while the majority of professional golfers will admit that building a classic swing and searching for the perfect strike isn't necessarily what golf's all about, it's what they spend all of their practice time working for.

PSYCHO-SICK

'There's nothing wrong with me, why do I need to see a psychologist?'

This is a comment I have overheard on several occasions. For many people, to be seen working on their mental skills is tantamount to admitting that there's something wrong with them. This attitude prevails in spite of the fact that many well-known professional golfers, not to mention successful athletes in other fields, are openly publicising the fact that it has helped them. Some people would rather not let anyone else know that they work on their mental game.

But think about it. If we're unwell, we go to see a doctor. And if we are keen to get physically fit, we seek the advice of an exercise physiologist. The same logic applies if we want to become mentally fit. If we are mentally sick we would see a psychiatrist, but if we want to become super-fit mentally, we seek the help of a sports psychologist.

TEACHER-CENTRED LEARNING

Sometimes the way we are taught is a factor in making it difficult to perform. I'll give you an example.

I started my career as a tennis coach. One of the problems I encountered on a regular basis was this. I would instruct some people how to play a particular shot, let's say a backhand, and they

The effect that our thinking has on our behaviour – and consequently on our performance – can be illustrated by this simple experiment. Take a piece of string between 12 and 18 inches (30 and 45 cm) long, attach a weight such as a bulldog clip to one end and hold it out in front of your body. Then, keeping the weight as steady as possible, picture in your mind the bulldog clip moving back and forth in a simple pendulum movement. If you have vividly imagined the pendulum motion you will find that the bulldog clip has begun to move in exactly the way you had imagined even though you thought you were keeping it steady. (Now imagine it moving in anti-clockwise circles). In other words, whatever you think about will be represented physically in some way. So, whenever you say to yourself 'Don't go in the water on the right ...'

would do just as I asked. I would give other people exactly the same instruction and it seemed to make them worse! And yet I knew it was the correct instruction, so I would tell them again and give them even more instructions. And they would get even worse. They were so busy thinking about all the things they had to do to play the backhand that the ball had gone by before they even started their swing. So then I would decide that they just weren't cut out to play the game. In other words, it was their fault!

I was wrong. The problem was not theirs, it was mine. I was so obsessed with my way of doing things on the tennis court that I wasn't interested in how my pupils learned. My lessons centred around what I wanted them to do as a teacher, not what they needed as a student to be able to learn effectively.

If you have had golf lessons from a number of different professionals, you have probably had a similar experience in some of those lessons.

What opened my eyes was applying one of the techniques Timothy Gallwey talks about in his *Inner Game* books. I had been teaching a 9-year-old girl for about six weeks. In that time her best back-and-forth rally with me on the practice court was just six consecutive strokes. I had kept the technical instruction very simple for her because she didn't seem to be particularly coordinated, and it had taken her several half-hour lessons to get even this far.

Sensing that my normal method of coaching was proving difficult for her to follow, I decided to try out one of Gallwey's techniques. I asked her to forget everything I had told her so far, and instead simply say 'bounce' out loud every time the ball bounced on the court, and 'hit' every time the ball hit her racket. The results were astonishing. She did 53 consecutive shots in her first rally. She was thrilled, her mother had almost fallen off her seat and I was furious! I didn't understand why this had worked and I was confused as to why what I had taught her up to now had had so little effect in comparison.

STOP! WARNING!

Reading this book will not make you a better golfer! In fact, reading any book will not make you a better golfer. We all know people who seem to have read every word ever written on golf and yet who have made little — if any — improvement.

If you think that simply by reading this book you will become a better golfer, then you will be disappointed. While the subject and

Bounce-hit?

In his book The Inner Game of Tennis, *Timothy Gallwey explains the concept of 'bounce-hit', a concentration exercise that he found greatly improved the performance and accelerated the learning rate of tennis players.*

The pupil was asked to say out loud the word 'bounce' as the approaching ball landed, and 'hit' when he felt the ball make contact with the racket. The object of the exercise was simply to maintain sensory contact with the ball and to say 'bounce-hit, bounce-hit' aloud with as much accuracy as possible — 'bounce' when the ball landed, and 'hit' when he struck it with his racket. Gallwey noted that the more attention that was given to saying 'bounce' and 'hit', the less his students consciously thought about their technique and the more successful they were in returning the ball. It allowed their subconscious to let them do what they already knew how to. (A comparable 'back-hit' exercise for golf is described on page 95.) Later I began to understand how the exercise regulated the mental state and that the mental state drives the physical action. I had made my first steps towards 'student-centred' learning.

content of the following chapters are going to be centred around developing the mental skills, you still need to understand the physical techniques of the game. But you can get that from many good sources. This book is based on the notion that in our search for bodily control – which is the essence of golf – we must complement our need for technical instruction with increased mental awareness. Only when we can harness the two are we likely to improve significantly.

The purpose of this book is to provide some insight into the mental aspects of playing this addictive game. And by the way, only doing the exercises and suggestions will make any difference. Just reading them won't!

Summary

- A major part of golf is mental.

- We don't practise mental skills in proportion to how important we think they are.

- Reasons for this include:
  Being obsessed with technique;
  Avoiding 'mental things';
  Our ignorance of the way we learn.

- Reading this won't make you play better, only taking action will.

MENTAL SKILLS

2

All of us have a mental state that affects our performance. The more we can develop our skill at controlling that mental state, the better we will perform all of our other skills.

WHAT ARE MENTAL SKILLS?

Mental skills are the internal skills that enable us to perform successfully the technical skills (physical skills) that we have already stored within our subconscious, or to learn those new skills that we wish to store in our subconscious. Examples of these mental skills are concentration (our ability to focus our attention), energy control (being 'pumped-up' or 'psyched-up'), self-confidence (self belief) and our ability to use our imagination effectively (the ability to visualise). The degree of skill which we have in each of these specific areas is reflected in our body language and in the words that we use, but most of all, it is reflected in our physical performance.

We use our mental skills in every area and in every minute of our lives. In whatever we do it is our brain that drives our behaviour, and therefore our brain that is responsible for our performance. Our brain 'houses' the mental skills we have; it sorts and interprets the stimuli that we receive through our senses – i.e. what we see, hear and feel – and on the basis of this interpretation, the brain drives what we do physically.

What most people fail to realise is that it is possible to train these inner skills. In the same way that we can design specific exercises to help us improve our swing technique, we can devise ways of improving our mental skills, and as a result improve our performance. In fact, it's sometimes easier to improve our mental skills than our physical skills, as the exercises that are shown later in this book can be practised off the golf course as well as on it.

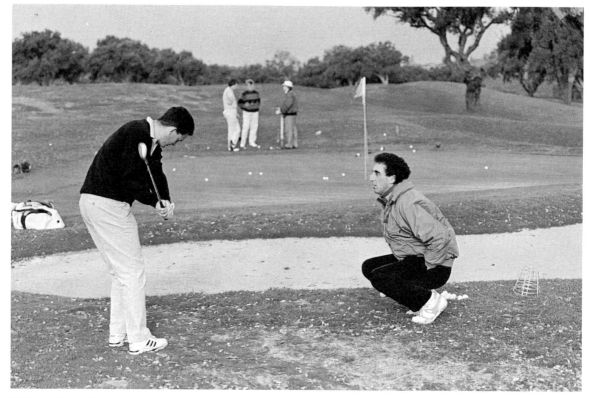

William Guy with the author,
sharpening his mental skills

THE BRAIN AND PERFORMANCE

In golf it is very easy to get caught up in the purely technical aspects
of the game. Although it is essential that we apply some quality
practice in this area, if that is all we do, we are ignoring what it is
that controls our technique. It's like spending all of our spare time
and money on building a high performance sports car, using all the
latest technology and tuning it to perfection, only to let a monkey
take the controls and drive it on the road when it really matters.
When we fail to learn the basic mental skills in golf, we are doing the
equivalent of allowing a monkey to drive our swings – and we occa-
sionally see this reflected in our behaviour out on the golf course!

Our brain controls everything we do. As far as I can tell, it is
not possible to split golf into separate mental and physical elements.
The two are so inextricably linked that whenever we deal with one
we have no choice but to deal with the other. To improve our
performance in any activity it can be enormously helpful to understand how our brain works, and what we can do to make it work
more efficiently. The more we understand the mechanism by which
we learn and perform, the better equipped we will be to cope with
the information that we have to deal with and act upon.

LEARNING

In my search for clues to improving performance, I have found it helpful to think about learning and performance in different ways. As yet we know so little about how our brains work that it isn't possible to be definitive, but suffice it to say that different people relate to words and concepts in differing ways (we will discuss this in more detail later). The following descriptions show the way in which I currently see the process of learning and performance unfolding.

LEARNING, UNDERSTANDING OR BOTH

One of the most common blocks to learning that I am familiar with is the confusion that surrounds the difference between 'learning' and 'understanding'. Often, what happens in golf is that we confuse understanding what to do with the ability to act on or implement that understanding. In other words, we tend to believe that the more we understand the 'what to do', then the more we will have learned and the more we will be able to do.

The 'what to do' in golf is the mass of information that is available to us on how to play the game – the detailed theory explaining all the body movements that are necessary to return the clubface to the ball in the most effective way. But simply reading and understanding this information – whether it's describing the grip, the posture or the backswing – is very different from actually being able to do it. Learning is not simply understanding; learning is experiencing a concept to the point of being able to execute that concept – that's how it becomes a skill.

Think about it this way. A pilot could explain to us how to fly an aeroplane, but while we might understand what he is saying, we certainly won't have learned how to fly. The only way we will ever do that is to get out and physically experience what is involved.

If we confuse learning with understanding, when we find we are unable to perform as we would ideally like to, we are inclined to go off in search of more 'how to' instruction. We want to know exactly what it is we are doing wrong and what we need to do to put it right. However, most of us already have all the technical information that we will ever need in order to play well (some of us have too much, others have the wrong information, and some both). It is not that we don't understand what to do, it is simply that we are not sufficiently skilled in acting on the information that we have.

It is not the player who knows where the club should be who is successful; it is the player who knows where the club is.

Guru Feherty (pre-1991 Ryder Cup)

The Description is NOT the Experience

Imagine that you are training for a parachute jump. You've been to the classes, and you've read all that there is to read about parachuting. Yet you still have no idea of what it is like actually to do it. It is impossible to know without doing it because words cannot give you the experience. So it is with golf.

LEARNING IS IN-BUILT

Psychologists tell us that we learn a half of what we learn in our whole lifetime in our first five years. So why does our rate of learning slow down so much after these first few years?

As children we had a tremendous capacity and appetite to learn, it was in-built at birth and is part of being human. We experienced the first years of our lives without preconceived ideas about what was right or wrong, or good or bad, or what we should or should not do. We had little or no fear or inhibition. During our formative years we developed our basic motor-skills through a very natural process, one that was free of formal instruction or training. We learned how to walk and to talk, to eat with a knife and fork, to run up and down stairs, and so on.

When attempting something as young children, our reaction would be along the lines of 'Oh, that's what happens. That's interesting. I wonder what happens if I try to do it this way ...' We were inquisitive. We did not judge our performances other than to decide what to do differently the next time in order to get what we wanted. Everything that we did was new and exciting. Our minds were relaxed, and learning was fun.

The way in which children learn is epitomised in their reaction to failure. When a child falls while learning to walk he doesn't react by saying to himself 'You dummy, you fell over. Why don't you try to keep your head still and keep your balance. Come on, try harder.' Children don't recognise failure. They just pick themselves up and try again.

Then, somewhere between the age of about five and seven years, we began to understand the concepts of right and wrong, good and bad, should and shouldn't. As a result we focused a lot of our energy and attention on avoiding the 'bad', the 'wrong' and the 'shouldn'ts', because we found that the consequences of these could be painful, or threaten us in some way. Our efforts were now directed into avoiding failure as distinct from learning.

By the time we reach adulthood, many of us are so fixated on there being a right and wrong way of doing things that we end up blocking our natural ability. We judge and evaluate our performance against some blue-print that we think will fix the problem. The potential for learning remains within us all, but as we grow older we tend to adopt a very analytical 'left-brained' (see Chapter Three) approach to learning which actually slows down the process of improving.

You are probably familiar with the symptoms. Our minds become so full of complicated and confusing instructions (keep your grip pressure light … keep your head still … turn your shoulders … etc.) that we stifle our natural instincts, and distort our perception of what's really happening as we are trying to play. If we had tried to follow similarly detailed instructions when we were children learning to walk, or ride a bicycle, it would have been much less effective.

And yet this is exactly how we go about learning to play golf, and in doing so, we eliminate that invaluable period of trial and error without the pressure of evaluation, or having to do it right. This is such a valuable part of the learning process – a time of working things out for ourselves and attaching feelings and meanings to our perceptions and actions.

IS GOLF NATURAL?

People have often said to me: 'But surely you have to do this analysis. After all, the golf swing is not a natural thing to do.' Well, no and yes. No, you don't need all of that information (but you do need some) and yes, golf isn't natural. **But learning is.** It is an in-built mechanism that exists in all of us, and the more we understand about how each of us likes to learn, the easier it will be to accelerate our learning and improve our results.

PERCEPTION: THE KEY TO LEARNING AND PERFORMANCE

It is through our perception that we know there is a world out there. We gather detailed information about our surroundings through our senses – i.e. what we see, hear, feel, taste and smell. That's how we make sense of the world in which we live and what we do in it. Similarly, we are aware of what we are doing on the golf course by seeing, feeling and hearing (taste and smell don't have much relevance in golf – at least not until the 19th hole!). We see the ball at our feet, for example, we observe the shape of the hole, the position of the bunkers and the proximity of the trees. We feel the way in which our bodies move before, during and after a shot, and we feel the wind and wonder how it will affect our stroke. At the same time we hear the swish of the club as it swings through the air and we hear the voices of other people.

All these senses are external to us, but we also have an internal

Stairclimbing –
Read with Care

Most of us have climbed stairs two at a time without any problem. We have also experienced those occasions when for some reason we thought about what we were doing, hesitated and then stumbled. We can do it easily and automatically all the time until we begin to think about it.

31

I think therefore I do

world that we see, hear and feel. We each have a set of beliefs that are based upon our expectations of future events, and on memories of past events when we were in a similar situation. And just as the external stimuli that we experience will have an effect on our interpretation of any given situation, so these internal stimuli shape our perception and therefore our reaction.

In our mind we see our prediction of the events to come, or our memories of the past. For example, we think about what will happen to the shot after we strike the ball, or about what happened the last time we were in a similar situation. When we stand on the first tee at our home course we might see what we hope will happen – the ball flying straight up the middle of the fairway – or we may see what we fear might happen – the ball disappearing into the trees as happened last time.

Similarly, we feel our prediction of the events to come or our memories of the past. We might feel the smoothness of our swing or the elation in response to a good shot; if we anticipate a poor shot we might feel uncomfortable or awkward over the ball, or disappointed. We also hear our prediction of the events to come or our memories of the past. If we anticipate success we might hear the crack of the ball as it is met squarely and forcefully by the clubface; if we anticipate failure that sound might be a muffled thud as the club strikes the ground behind the ball.

In golf there are an infinite variety of sights, sounds, and feelings that we experience whenever we are playing. Later we will discuss in more detail the value of identifying those particular sights, sounds and feelings that we associate with success.

THE PERFORMANCE LOOP

Think about the process of generating performance as a closed loop, in which both external and internal stimuli play a part in determining our brain's interpretation to a situation and therefore our physical response to it (see diagram below). This loop starts with the external event, or action, that we perceive through our senses – i.e. our sight, sound and touch. That is interpreted by our brain and the sensory experience together with the interpretation is what is called perception. Our brain then initiates a response to its interpretation – i.e. we re-act. We then experience our reaction through our senses, and start back through the loop all over again.

You will notice in the diagram that a lens is drawn in front of the brain. If our mind is quiet we hardly know this lens is there.

The performance loop

The stimuli that come into our brains from our senses are 'focused' by the lens so that we get a high quality 'image', and the result is that we get a high quality reaction to this 'image' or interpretation.

We all have beliefs (or paradigms) about ourselves, or about our golf, or both. These beliefs affect our perception, filtering the stimuli coming into our brain. Our beliefs are like dirt on the lens in the loop. When the stimuli that we are sensing hit a belief, we cannot be sure that it will come straight through the lens and form an accurate image for our brain to interpret. From this inaccurate image we form an inaccurate interpretation – the mental state causes the physical response. The stronger the belief, the more dense the 'dirt' on our lens is, and the more distorted the information coming through becomes.

Depending on how well we manage our mental state, these beliefs can work for us ('I can do it!') or against us ('I'm not good enough to do it'). But in golf, my experience is that more often than not our perception works against us. The beliefs that we have tend to act as a filter, and adversely affect the quality of the sensory information that we need in order to control our actions and form rational conclusions.

Generally speaking, our learning and performance improves the more fully we experience what it is we are doing, and so one way to improve the efficiency of this loop is simply to *clean our lens,* i.e. change or remove our beliefs, so that our processing mechanism gets only the information it needs in order to form the right conclusions. That is what the focusing exercises that we will come to later are designed to do.

When we hit a bad shot it means that we didn't swing correctly, that our actions were not the right ones. This does not happen spontaneously; it is caused by an inappropriate mental state which generated an inappropriate or inaccurate swing. Of course, the mental state might be triggered by some action. So now we have a chicken and egg situation – which comes first? As yet I don't know. But what matters to me is what can I do about it. And we are coming to that soon!

Give them a hammer, and all they see are nails ...

When we consider buying a new car, once we have decided on the model we want to buy, that model is all we see on the road from then on.

THE BRAIN DRIVES OUR BODY

Our brain is like an engine room that drives our behaviour, constantly receiving sensory stimuli which we then sort and interpret according to our individual characteristics. These characteristics are different in all of us, and they reflect our own individual beliefs and our

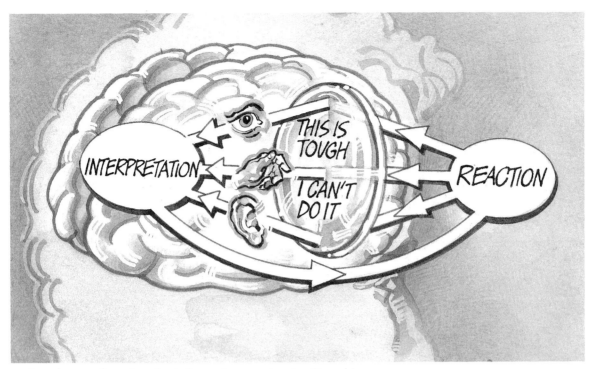

preferred way of sorting the information coming in. One thing we all have in common is that our physical performance is always related to our conclusions or interpretations, whatever they may be.

In other words, we always act in response to (or in a way that represents) the content of our thinking (or perception).

THINKING → ACTION.

Generally speaking, the better the quality with which we experience something, the more effective our learning and performance is. Problems arise when our experience is clouded, either by our interpretation of the external stimuli (i.e. what we see, hear and feel), or by our interpretation of the internal stimuli (what our beliefs tell us). (See diagram above.)

ONE WORLD – TWO PERCEPTIONS

People can and do interpret the same information in the external world in many different ways. We have all been to different golf professionals for lessons and wondered why it is that they all say something different. Rarely are we given the same advice twice, and yet they are all looking at the same swing – ours! The advice they give is genuine; however, they each have a different interpretation of what they see in our swing and this prompts them to give different advice.

One Man's Threat ...

When Ian Woosnam stands on the tee at the 17th at St Andrews, he perceives it as a tough hole but a relatively comfortable first shot for him. He plays with a natural draw which enables him to deal more easily with the out-of-bounds down the right hand side. When you and I stand on this infamous Road Hole, we probably perceive a hole fraught with danger. It is the same hole so who's right?

The infamous Road Hole at St Andrews

Sometimes things aren't what
they seem ...

Although external reality might appear to be the same for everyone, it is our perception as an individual that establishes how this reality is interpreted. We each have a unique way of identifying and organising information according to our past experiences, our current knowledge, and our future expectations. An event is therefore not only perceived, but also interpreted, in accordance with our moods, our feelings, the memories it evokes, the thoughts it triggers off, and the hopes and fears that it may cause. These factors all contribute to our mental condition, and therefore affect our action.

... the green can seem like a postage stamp.
The Emirates Course in Dubai

THREATS AND OPPORTUNITIES

Let's explore in more detail the notion that it is our thinking, or mental state, that drives our performance.

When I'm working with a group of mixed ability golfers, I sometimes ask the experienced players to explain to the beginners the basics of the game in terms of what they need to do to swing a golf club. They usually give some form of the following in reply:

'Hold the club with your right hand below your left ...'

'Make sure that the "V" that is formed between the thumb and

index finger of each hand points up towards your right shoulder as you hold the club ...'

'Stand with your feet comfortably apart, and place the ball somewhere between the middle of your stance and your left heel ...'

'Make sure that the clubface is square to the ball at address ...'

'Bend from the hips and flex your knees ...'

'Take the club back smoothly, keeping your left arm reasonably straight ...'

'Keep your head still ...'

'Keep the club on the correct plane ...'

I then ask the beginners in the group what this all sounds like to them. 'Difficult' is the usual reply.

When we perceive something as being difficult our usual response is to try harder to do that thing – here it is swinging the golf club. When we try harder, we tighten our muscles and that makes it more difficult to coordinate, so we are more likely to make an error. And when we make an error we say to ourselves 'That was difficult, I'd better try even harder.' We get caught in a vicious circle.

We perceive the challenge confronting us as too great for the skills that we think we have. This induces worry and then anxiety (see diagram on page 42), and in this condition our mental state is not conducive to creating our best performances or the learning of new skills.

I then reverse the process and ask the beginners to tell the experienced golfers what to do, and the task they set is usually very simple. Whatever the beginners tell the pros, the pros respond by saying 'that's too easy, it would be boring'. They now perceive the skill that they possess as being much greater than the challenge they are faced with. The consequences of them trying to practise those instructions also show up in the diagram.

We can see from the diagram on page 42 that if we keep the challenge facing us in balance with the skill that we have, we are much more likely to achieve the flow or optimum mental state. (The exercises later in this book are designed to do just that.)

MENTAL STATE AND PEAK PERFORMANCE

In trying to understand what influences those rare moments of peak performance, sports psychologist James Loehr studied over 200 athletes. He discovered that their highest levels of performance

Walking the Plank

Imagine walking along a 4-inch wide plank laid out across the floor. We would have very little trouble doing this. Now imagine what it would be like to walk this same plank when it is 5 feet off the ground. Now we would be much more careful, hesitant and tight with every step we made. It is the same task but we perceive it in very different ways and our actions in response to our perception create very different results.

opposite: The balance of challenge and skill – in action

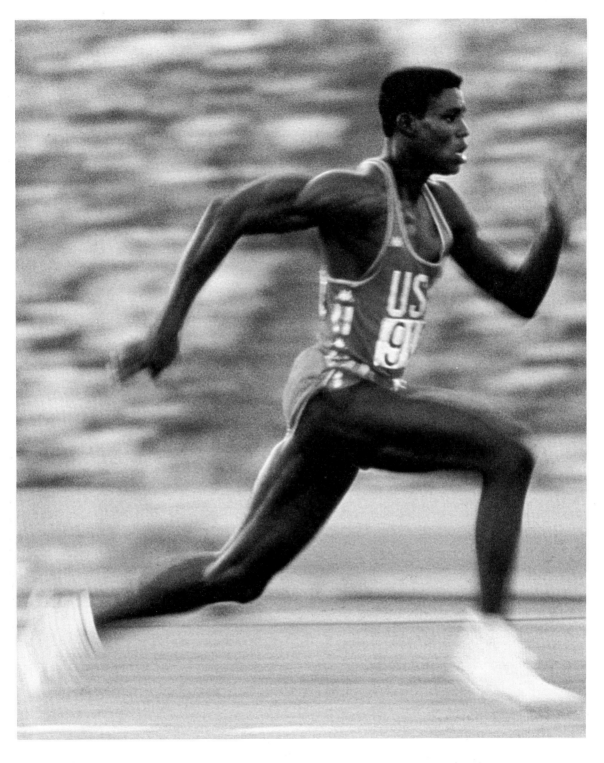

Carl Lewis often illustrates a
positive mental attitude

MENTAL STATE DETERMINES PERFORMANCE

Mental state for
peak performance

HIGH ENERGY

Moderate to poor

Alert	Calm mental state	Fearful	Accelerated mental state
Lively		Anxious	Tense
Stimulated	Relaxed concentration	Angry	Tunnel vision
Enthused	Focused	Frustrated	

'I can do it..'

'I want to, but I'm afraid
I won't be able to.'

No threat   **Threat**

**POSITIVE
ATTITUDE
PLEASANT**

**NEGATIVE
ATTITUDE
UNPLEASANT**

'I want to, but not
all that much.'

No threat   **Mild threat**

'I'd rather be doing
anything else but…'

Fatigued	Calm mental state	Bored	Variable calmness
Lazy		Uninterested	
Leisurely	No tension	Irritated	Some tension
Lackadaisical	Unfocused	Depressed	Unfocused

Poor

LOW ENERGY

Very poor

occurred most often when they had a high level of energy coupled with a positive mental attitude (see diagram opposite). On the basis of his research, Loehr concluded that the ideal mental condition for peak performance is one which features a calm mind, relaxed muscles and focused attention. In this state we say to ourselves 'I can do it'.

We believe that the skill that we think we have is in balance with the challenge we are engaging in (see diagram opposite).

Loehr found that when people are negative in their attitude but high in energy, they are much less likely to achieve peak performance. In this situation we are inclined to say to ourselves 'I want to, but I'm afraid I won't be able to do it' (see diagram on page opposite).

We feel threatened because the challenge we think we are faced with appears to be much greater than the skill we think we have.

Loehr also found that when people are both negative in their attitude and low in energy, they are much less likely to achieve peak performance.

He established that the optimum mental attitude preceded high performance – not the other way around.

In other words, the mental state came before and facilitated the performance. We all recognise that if we play well, our energy goes up and we feel good, but it can be much easier to raise the energy and create focus in order to play better than it is to play better in order to feel good. That, of course, is what this book is about.

THE GOLFER'S NIGHTMARE – TRYING TOO HARD

Trying too hard is such a common phenomenon in golf that it's worth spending a little more time on it.

We are taught from birth that we must try as hard as we can to achieve our goals, and on the whole this is very commendable. But try the arm-bending exercise shown in the diagram! Here, the harder you tried, the worse your performance. When you seemingly tried less hard, it became much easier to keep your arm straight.

We have probably all experienced this phenomenon at work in our golf. We are out on the practice range with a driver, trying to hit the ball as far as we can – let's say 250 yards. And, although we've been trying very hard to hit the ball a long way, our best effort has only just crossed the 200-yard marker. There are only six balls left, so we give up. We decide to relax and just enjoy hitting them; we're not trying to hit them a long way or think very much

Our perception affects our performance – in anything

For many people (especially me), making a speech in front of an audience is a nerve-racking experience. We are often anxious, particularly when we doubt our ability to perform the task well. These feelings are usually accompanied by physical reactions. Our throat feels 'tight', and our mouth gets dry. When we start to speak, the words come out in a strangled fashion due to the tension in our throats. Our minds become busy with thoughts about what the audience will think of us and it becomes difficult to organise in our mind what we want to say. The words come out jumbled and we are hesitant. We see the audience begin to fidget and one or two even start to talk amongst themselves. They fold their arms and we decide they are not impressed with what we have to say. So we try harder and tighten even more. This causes our voices to croak even more. The audience senses this and appears even more uncomfortable.

We have the vicious circle of belief, action based on belief, and perceived reaction of audience reinforcing our belief.

Hold one arm straight out in front of you. Ask a friend to put one hand in the crook of your elbow and the other hand under your wrist and then to try to bend your arm at the elbow (1). Your job is to resist as hard as you can without moving. Both of you need to gauge how much effort you need to use in order to do your respective tasks.

Then ask your friend to do exactly the same again. This time imagine that you have a beam of light (like a laser beam) coming out of your fingers. Imagine the beam hitting the wall, or whatever it is pointing at and imagine smoke coming out of the hole it is burning, with flames and fire etc. Ignore what your partner is doing as he tries to bend your arm again (2).

In figure 1 you are in the mental state of trying hard, but you are using the wrong muscles, and it will be hard work to keep your arm from bending. But when you keep your mind fully focused on the light beam, as in figure 2, you change your mental state to one of focused attention and it becomes easier to keep your arm straight and harder for your partner to bend it.

Trying hard needs to be directed in the right area to be really effective.

about what we're doing technically. We're simply having fun. And what happens? Our muscles relax, we coordinate our swing much better and generate the clubhead speed that's necessary to hit the ball a long way. Suddenly we realise that we've just hit one past the 250-yard marker, and we say to ourselves, 'That's it. I've got it. I'll try to do that again.' And as soon as we say that to ourselves, we're right back where we started. Our mental state is back in the 'trying too hard' mode, our muscles tighten and our ability to create clubhead speed is lost.

EXPERIENCE, LEARNING AND PERFORMANCE

In his work on the *Inner Game of Golf*, Timothy Gallwey describes a relationship between experience, learning and performance that sparked some investigation on my part.

I had always wondered why it was that beginners seemed to improve very quickly during their first few months, but then reach a plateau in terms of their progress. As I began to do more work in golf I noticed a pattern emerging, one that seemed to reflect the relationship that Gallwey had identified between experience, learning and performance.

It would appear to me that people take up golf for a number of different reasons, including:

- the challenge of the game
- to get exercise
- the peace and quiet
- to be with family and/or friends
- to be away from family and/or friends
- to prove themselves

Whatever our reason, we usually derive some form of enjoyment from the game. As beginners, we had few expectations of playing well. In other words, we had a very easy-going and relaxed attitude – one similar to the peak performance state discussed earlier – and this in turn caused our performance to rise very rapidly.

Then other people began to notice our improvement, and would say things like 'Aren't you doing well, you've improved tremendously …' And naturally we enjoyed all the praise and attention. It satisfied our ego and obviously meant that we were doing something right.

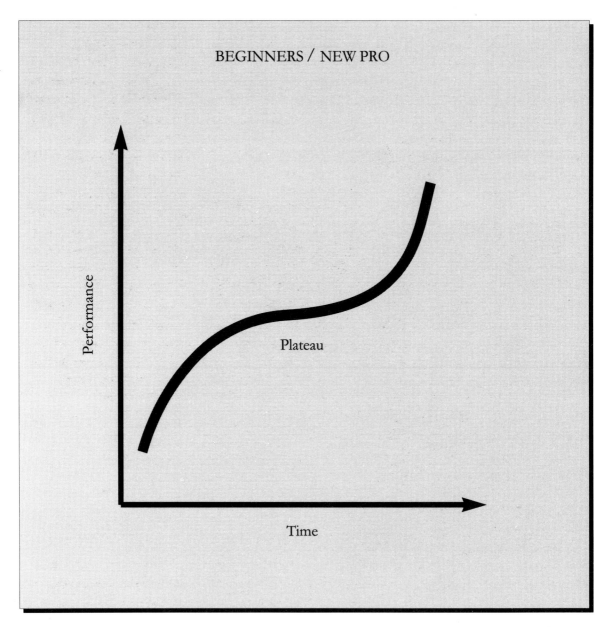

BEGINNERS / NEW PRO

Performance

Plateau

Time

We began to look forward to the compliments and the flattering remarks about our performance, and slowly (and without realising it) our attention shifted away from simply playing as a means of enjoyment to trying to ensure that we did not play any worse than before. In other words, our attention became caught up on our performance, on trying to maintain a standard rather than experiencing what we were doing. And our performance and learning dropped dramatically as a result (see diagram above). Of course, we eventually pass through this stage, and start improving again.

*The Ryder Cup in 1991
produced some pretty
spectacular collapses, most
notably that perpetrated by the
American Mark Calcavvechia
who, having been 5 up on Colin
Montgomerie after 9 holes,
found himself dragged back to
2 up with two to play at
Kiawiah. I watched anxiously
as Montgomerie dunked his tee-
shot in the water at the par-3
17th, only to be followed by
Calcavvechia, who would have
closed the match there and then
had he simply carried the water
with his tee-shot. Instead he
played one of the worst shots
of his career, and Montgomerie
went on to secure the most
unlikely of halves.*

Ryder Cup 91. Calcavecchia and
Montgomerie

The next time I saw this happen was with golfers who had just
turned professional. Again, the emphasis changed from experiencing
and learning to performance. The justification this time is 'Now it
is serious. My living depends on it'. They are right, of course, their
living does depend on it, but approaching the game with this attitude
sends the wrong stimuli into the performance loop, and as a result
we get the wrong output. Experience is what teaches us how to do
what we want to do, or know we should do.

H.E.L.P.

This is an acronym that I use in training coaches which may be just as relevant to us as players. It represents:

intensify
to increase
and raise

H elp
E xperience
L earning
P erformance

In the performance loop our interpretation is based on what we experience, and this experience is based on a combination of our beliefs and the sensory input from the external world. Remember, what we experience is the external stimuli filtered through our beliefs. Our problem is that often the stimuli that eventually get through our beliefs represent an inaccurate picture of the external world. But they are the stimuli that we respond to, the ones that drive our behaviour and therefore our performance.

The more we can intensify our experience of events, or the more we are aware of what we are doing, the more we learn (i.e. change our behaviour) and therefore the better our performance becomes. It goes in that order. This does not mean that we must consciously know everything about what we are doing at all times. As we discovered with the pendulum and arm-bending experiments, our subconscious is a very powerful tool if we feed it the right information. Input the right stimuli and you get the right output. Input the wrong stimuli and you get the wrong output. It's a simple equation. As they say in computing, garbage in = garbage out.

The trick is to increase your understanding of what stimuli to feed into the performance loop, and how to feed these in so that we get the output or performance that we want.

MENTAL INTERFERENCE

Timothy Gallwey coined the phrase 'mental interference' in his inner game books. He suggests that a player's performance at any given moment is equal to his capacity to perform (i.e. his current level of ability) less the interference present (i.e. the things that distract his attention). This interference can be either external or internal. In golf, external interferences would include the weather, the condition of the course, the presence of spectators or even the performance of our opponent. Internal interferences, on the other hand, are the

BEGINNERS / NEW PRO

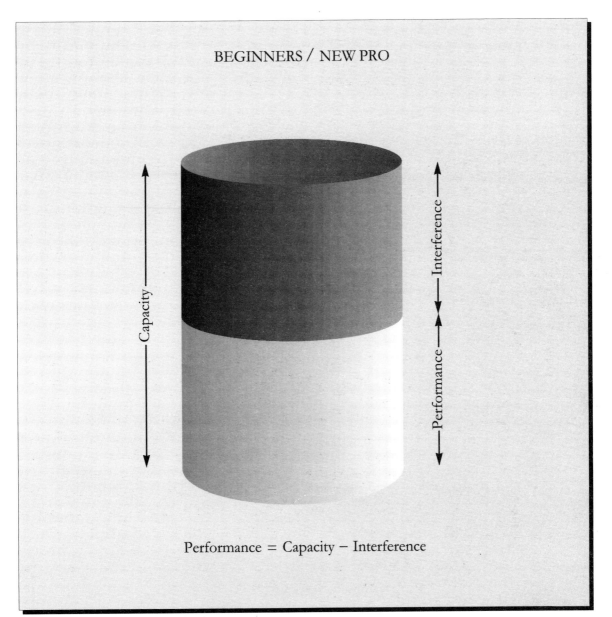

Performance = Capacity − Interference

distractions that are already firmly implanted in our mind, a constant stream of internal chatter. Internal interference is often the more powerful, and is caused by:

- **the ego (expectations, perfectionism, self-consciousness)**
- **lack of self-confidence, fear, or self-condemnation.**
- **false assumptions**

Fear can be a real dilemma for the golfer. At its worst, it manifests itself in what are called the yips – a jerky, erratic movement that can send the ball in all directions. Our perception of the threat

Langer. Last hole, last putt, Ryder
Cup 91. If it's in we retain the
Cup. Could the interference be
any greater?

Assumptions. Sit down with your eyes closed and raise your arms
out in front of you so that one points upwards at 45 degrees
and one points downwards at 45 degrees. Hold this for 30
seconds and then put both arms horizontally out in front of you
parallel with the ground without opening your eyes. As soon as
you have done that open your eyes and see what you have done.

facing us is so frightening that it evokes what psychologists call the
'flight or fight' response. Yipping usually refers to a golfer's putting
stroke, but it is possible to identify the same symptoms in any part
of the game (fear of bunkers, chipping, pitching etc).

Imagine getting ready to hit a 3-foot putt to win the monthly
medal or a cheque for £50,000 (it's not the amount that matters
here, it's our perception of the challenge we face). If we perceive
the challenge as being way too much for our skill – which a 3-foot
putt to someone who has the yips would be – we get ready for
action that would deal with a huge threat. Given the performance
loop, we will respond to our interpretation according to our experience of the events, and the way in which we experienced the stimuli
would tell us that we are in danger. Under this kind of threat our
bodies automatically pump more blood into the large muscles and
put more adrenaline into our system to get us ready to either fight
the threat or run from it. However, we don't want this kind of
response in golf, particularly when we are putting, because it causes
large, powerful, but inappropriate muscle movements, and we need
small fine movements to putt accurately.

Making assumptions about where our body is in space is a frequent cause of trouble in golf (as shown in the exercise opposite). If we are unable to tell whether our hands are in one position or another, we are unlikely to be able to sense what position the clubhead is in either. If we think the clubhead is in position A, and it is actually in position B we have a problem – and it gets worse.

Let me give you an example. Imagine that we hit a ball and it flies off to the right. Now we already know what causes this because we've read about it, and the pro has confirmed that in our case one of the problems is the position of our hands at impact. So we consciously try to release our hands a little more forcefully through impact to get the clubface into the correct position to strike the ball. But the problem is not that we don't know what to do, it's that we can't tell with any accuracy where our clubface is in the first place – so how can we possibly expect to correct it? The trick is to increase our awareness of where the clubface actually is by experiencing it more fully.

BELIEFS

A crucial element in feeding the wrong stimuli into our performance loop are our beliefs. Beliefs are hard to define and recognise, yet they have a very powerful effect on our performance. Beliefs are things we think about the actual events that happen. They may or may not be accurate. They are not the events themselves.

Examples of the beliefs that affect our performance in golf are:

'I can't play out of sand.'
'I always slice.'
'They are better than I am.'
'My clubs aren't right.'
'I never have been very coordinated.'

Our beliefs act as filters to the information provided by our senses. They screen the information in a way that causes us to interpret the stimuli and react in a way that we don't really want. Let's take a typical example. I'd like you to meet Steven Slicer!

Steven begins his round fairly happy with his form, but on the 1st tee he carves his ball away into the rough beside the fairway. He watches the flight of the ball, and then says to himself 'I sliced that one'. He continues to play and minutes later does the same thing at the 3rd. This time he observes the slice, and then says 'I

> *The truth believed is a lie.*

Anon

am slicing today.' At the 6th he carves another one way into the trees on the right, and this time declares 'I have a slice today.' A little further into the round and our hero hits another terrible slice at the 14th, and this time concludes 'I am a slicer.' Then, on the 15th, he misses a short putt, and says 'I am no good at this game.'

Losing at squash the next day provokes the thought 'I am not very good at sports' and when things don't go right at work 'I am not a good person.'

And so Steven Slicer gets caught up in the performance loop in a very destructive way. It starts when he observes a slice. When he sees the second one go that way he decides that he may have a slice. The next one he sees reinforces his belief that he has this problem, and now he's looking out for the thing he fears most – another slice! This causes him to try not to slice, which causes tension, locking the clubface and causing even more slice. When it happens again, he turns to his partners and celebrates 'That's me, you see. I told you I always slice the ball.'

His belief becomes so strong that on the rare occasions when he does hit the ball straight he just says to himself (and others) 'Oh, that's just lucky. I can't really do that.' This way he can ignore the evidence that contradicts his belief that he is a slicer. And the more he tries to prevent his slice, the worse it inevitably gets.

Summary

- The brain drives what we do physically.

- Mental skills enable us to perform the technical skills.

- Our response to any given situation is determined by how accurately we perceive reality.

- Mental interference prevents us from accurately perceiving reality.

- Intensifying our experience reduces interference, increases our learning and improves our performance.

TWO BRAINS, THREE SENSES – MORE ABOUT HOW WE WORK

3

Those of us who studied human biology in school will remember being taught that the brain has two hemispheres, the left hemisphere and the right hemisphere. We may have been taught that these different hemispheres control different aspects of our functioning as human beings. What I certainly wasn't taught was how significant the different ways these hemispheres work is to our golf.

I was also taught that I have five senses. What we have learned since is that three of these senses play a vital role in our golf in terms of how we conceptualise or think about our golf (or anything for that matter) and how we perceive and act in the external world.

First, let's look at our two hemispheres or two brains.

RIGHT AND LEFT BRAINS?

There are three important things to note when we talk about the different halves of the brain:

1 They control different functions in us.
2 A lot of us tend to lean towards being more left- or more right-brained in our approach to golf and life generally.
3 Golf as an activity has some elements that demand the use of our left hemisphere, and other elements that demand more use of our right hemisphere.

"LEFT BRAINER"

NEAT
TIMELY
CRITICAL
ORGANIZES
ANALYTICAL
QUANTITATIVE
LIKES NUMBERS
GETS THINGS DONE
LIKES ROUTINES
KNOWS HOW
THINGS WORK
REALISTIC
RELIABLE
LOGICAL
PLANS

"RIGHT BRAINER"

FEELS
CURIOUS
IMPETUOUS
IMAGINATIVE
SPECULATIVE
BREAKS RULES
SENSITIVE TO OTHERS
LIKES SURPRISES
KINESTHETIC
TAKES RISKS
EMOTIONAL
PLAYFUL
GUESSES

Let me explain some more by comparing the differences between right-brain dominant people – described as 'right-brainers' – and left-brain dominant people – or 'left-brainers'.

Left-brainers are logical, timely, reliable, neat, realistic and analytical. They can be critical, they like things to be well planned and organised. They thrive on routine, will practise for hours and generally want to understand thoroughly before doing.

Right-brainers are imaginative, impetuous, take risks and break rules. They are holistic, good at conceptualising, intuitive, creative and sensitive. They are curious, like surprises, relate well to feel (are kinaesthetic), and enjoy movement.

Of course no one is totally right-brained or totally left-brained, but most of us tend to be more one way or the other. That makes it easier for us to learn or do the things that demand the use of the dominant half of our brain, and harder for us to learn or do the things that demand the use of the non-dominant half of our brain.

Bearing in mind the above, here is how we run into difficulties. Imagine that I tend to be more left-brained in my approach to life. I will tend to apply my left-brained approach to the whole of my golf, and I will perform well the elements of golf that demand the functions of my left brain. However, the elements that demand the use of my right brain will suffer, because I still try to apply my preferred left-brain mode of thinking. It's a bit like trying to screw in a normal slotted screw with a cross-headed screwdriver. It's the wrong tool for the job, and it makes life very difficult.

LEFT- OR RIGHT-BRAINED GOLF

Now think about golf. As an activity it has two distinct phases. The first phase is what I call the pre-swing, and it involves our activity before we hit the ball. It contains our arriving at the ball, analysing the situation we are faced with, working out the shot we need to make, assessing whether or not we have the skill to execute it, selecting a club for the job and beginning our routine, which would probably include carefully lining up.

The second phase comes once we have finished our pre-swing routine. This is the moment when we hit the ball. It is the time when we need to stop thinking and allow the pre-swing work we have been doing to have its effect. It is where we need to experience what we are actually doing. We have pointed our brains in the right direction and now we let our bodies get on with it.

If we refer back to the characteristics of left- and right-brained

The left brain at work

thinking, it's easy to see that our left brain is best suited to the first phase (pre-swing), while the right brain is best suited to the activities of the second phase (playing). The left brain is good at taking care of the analysis and decision making; the right brain is good at acting on that analysis and decision.

In my experience the dilemma for the majority of us is that we tend to take the left-brained approach into the right-brained orientated activities. We are still analysing and instructing ourselves in the moments when we need to be just doing, and experiencing what we are doing. The problem for many people is that trusting the right brain to take care of the physical action without conscious guidance can feel like taking a risk, that we have less control and that we are unsure what will happen next.

A significant number of us will also do the reverse – I'm one of them. Being right-brain dominant, I prefer to do something quite quickly before analysing it. So when I play golf I want to get on and hit the ball without analysing the situation properly and without going through a proper pre-shot routine.

It is important to realise that none of this is good or bad, or right or wrong. It is just how we are as human beings, and the better we understand our predispositions the better we can use them

The right brain at work

in our favour. By identifying which is the dominant half of our brain, we can work on developing the skills of our non-dominant half by practising activities that demand those skills. In my case, being a right-brained dominant thinker, I would improve my performance if I introduced a little more left-brain discipline into my game, and developed a specific pre-shot routine that helped me to eliminate elementary errors. A left-brainer, on the other hand, might learn to reduce the analysis and self-instruction, and let his subconscious get on with hitting the ball. The various focusing exercises that we will come to later are designed to eliminate this sort of internal interference (and can be applied both in practice and out on the course).

THE THREE SENSES – SEEING, FEELING AND HEARING

We said earlier that the way we know there is a world out there is through our senses, and that as there was not very much smelling and tasting to do in golf, the major senses that tell us about our golfing world are seeing, feeling and hearing. We experience, interpret and act on the stimuli that are relayed through our senses. These stimuli come to us in varying combinations of seeing (visual) data, kinaesthetic (feeling) data and auditory (hearing) data.

When we think about our golf, we think in terms of visual, kinaesthetic and auditory concepts. The concept in our mind may be visual – we may associate with, or form pictures in our mind about whatever we are thinking about. It may be kinaesthetic – we may associate with or form feelings in our mind about what we are thinking about. It may also be auditory – we may associate with or form sounds about what we are thinking about. Most of us will conceptualise using various amounts of all three.

It seems that we have the same mechanism at work whether we are sensing the outside world or our own internal world. We create our sense of meaning of the world by combining the input from these three senses.

However, we also have a specific sense that dominates our consciousness in telling us about the world, whether that world is our internal one or the external one. Just as we have a dominant right or left hemisphere in our brain, we have dominant sensory ways of thinking in each of these hemispheres. Using our dominant sensory mode can be as important as using the appropriate side of the brain for the right task in golf when we come to determining the keys to peak performance.

It is much easier for us to understand things that are described in our dominant mode. Some of us respond much more readily to visual language and/or communication. For example, we 'see the swing', or 'get the picture'. Some 'grasp the idea' or 'get a feel for it', While others 'hear what you mean' or 'get the rhythm' of the swing. Understanding which is our dominant mode (we also have secondary modes) can help speed up our learning process, make it easier to concentrate and help us be more reliable under pressure. The key to high performance and accelerated learning is to manage the stimuli coming into the performance loop, and understanding our dominant modes can help us do that.

The three senses: seeing, feeling and hearing

THE MANAGEMENT OF PERCEPTION

So what? So we have a dominant side to our brains. So we have a preferred sensory mode. What do we do with all this?

Remember it is our brain that drives or causes our action, and so it follows that the better we drive our brain, the better it will drive that action. And the brain is a superb mechanism. It learnt how to walk and talk long before you were able to tell it what and how to walk and talk – or swing a golf club. So, given the performance loop, we potentially have two places that we can exert some influence over things. One is our perception of the external world, and the other is our perception of our internal world, both of which go to make up our experience of the world as a whole. As we get into the exercises I will suggest some that help with one or the other, and some that work with both.

First, let's begin to think about which are our dominant modes. Read through these descriptions and decide which one is closest to you. We are not aiming to be statistically or psychologically accurate here, just to provide us with some food for thought.

RIGHT-BRAIN DOMINANT

When I play, I:

Like to imagine/create new shots
Am sometimes reckless in my choice of shot
Guess the yardage
Hit the ball in unconventional ways (when others think it's unnecessary)
Like to play the bold shot
Enjoy new courses and playing partners
Like to have fun when playing
Can tell when something is bothering other people and try to change it
Get the feel of things
Get highs and lows in response to how well I am doing
Am curious about other ways to achieve the end result

LEFT-BRAIN DOMINANT

When I play, I:

Like to analyse every swing I make, especially if it goes wrong
Want logical explanations for everything I do
Always arrive to play on time
Do what I say I will
Like routines
Am critical of myself (and others) if things are not right
Try to be realistic with my goals
Prefer practice that can be measured, quantified and analysed
Like to understand why I do things
Always dress neatly

Plan how I will play a hole

Organise my playing, practice and social schedule

Of course no one is totally one or the other of these, but most of us lean one way or another in our preferences. Some of us will lean only slightly one way. Others will be closer to one of the two extremes. If we are more right-brained in our preferences, then the pre-swing phase is where we can make a significant gain. If we are more left-brained in our preferences, then we have probably analysed our swing to death already. We will need to learn to let go of our thinking about the right way to do things while we make our swing.

SENSORY MODES

Learning which are our dominant modes takes time and is easier for some people to do than others. Some clues as to which might be our dominant sense are set out below.

If our dominant sensory mode is visual, we tend to notice or remember:

brightness or intensity

colour

size

location in space

shape

movement

We use words like 'see', 'perspective', 'point of view'. We talk faster than others, and wear bright, neat clothing. We learn easily from visual aids, walk quite quickly, watch television to relax, form first impressions of people and remember things by what they look like.

If our dominant mode is kinaesthetic, we tend to notice or remember:

bodily sensations

emotions

movement

temperature

pressure

humidity

texture

rhythm

balance

We use words like 'feel', 'grasp', 'get the hang of'. We have slower, deeper voices and dress casually and comfortably. We learn more easily from doing, we walk slowly, slouch in a chair to relax and respond to feelings – we are good empathisers.

If our dominant sensory mode is auditory, we tend to notice or remember these aspects of what we hear:

pitch
tone
clarity
duration
tempo
rhythm
loudness
location in space

We use words like 'hear', and phrases like 'that rings a bell', or 'the noise in my system'. We have rhythmic voices and learn better from people with good voices. We walk with a distinct rhythm, listen to music to relax, and are comfortable being on our own.

Some of you will recognise which of these applies most to you quite quickly, while others will find it much more difficult. There is no right preference to have, no dominant mode that will make you a better golfer. And no, you are not a hopeless case if you cannot immediately identify your dominant modes – it takes practice.

However, if there is a secret in golf, it lies in learning to manage our sensory modes and preferences in ways that produce the results that we want. At some time or another we have all played well or pulled off a spectacular shot, and when we did, the various facets of our mental state gelled together. What we need to do is identify what characterised this mental state, and look at ways of inducing it more often.

In the next chapter we will identify some ways to uncover our preferences and begin to manage our brains in ways that help us produce more of what we want more of the time.

DISCOMFORT

In my experience, one of the biggest problems that faces us when we want to improve is that we don't like to change. Many of us prefer to remain within our 'comfort' zone as we go about our

Golf provides some of the most
beautiful sporting environments
in the world. The Augusta
National course in Georgia (top)
and the Belfy near Sutton
Coldfield (below)

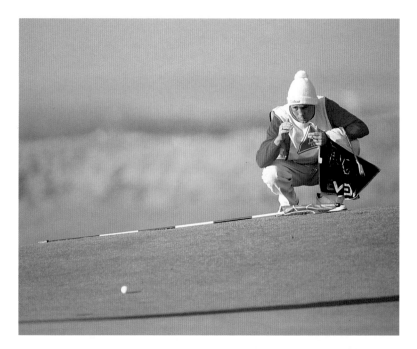

Concentration is available to
everyone (including the caddies)

David Feherty is so focussed that
he doesn't even notice the rain

Keeping their eyes on the ball.
Two of golf's greatest exponents:
Greg Norman (left) and Seve
Ballesteros (above)

Coping with pressure. The better
you get the more you face. David
Feherty reaches the 18th green at
the British Open in 1989

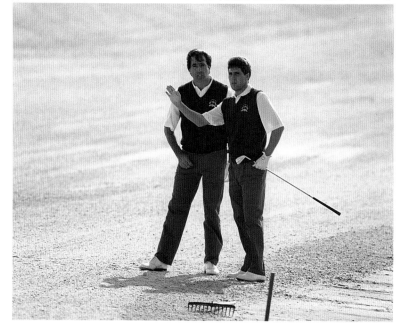

Golf also provides some unusual environments: Seve Ballesteros and Jose-Maria Olazabal at Kiawiah Island, Florida (right), Ian Woosnam also at Kiawiah (top) and Nick Faldo at Quiet Waters in Essex (above)

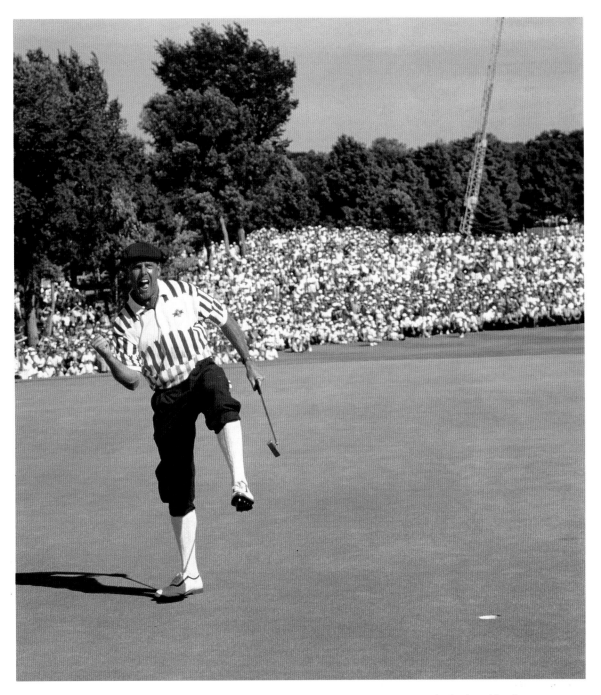

And when it's all over, we can celebrate ... (Payne Stewart)

... and celebrate ... (Laura
Davies)

... or even pray ... (Christy
O'Connor Jnr)

How we learn ... Another way
to think about it

learning, but doing this makes progress a very slow process. If we want to improve, we must be prepared to do something differently – to change what we do – and that means moving into our stretch zone (see skiing example). But change, for many of us, is an uncomfortable process, and to avoid this discomfort we often go back to doing what we are used to – old habits die hard. And, not surprisingly, we get the same old results. We always get the results of our actions. Always!

To encourage us to be willing to approach things differently, here is one more way to think about the learning process. It is not the truth. No model is. But it may simplify and therefore help us to understand how our performance happens. You will notice a process that goes on subconsciously that I have called 'integration' and 'execution'. We don't know it is happening because it is subconscious, but it happens none the less.

We always like to know what we are doing. Our egos like to be in charge, so much so that many of us find it very difficult just to allow this subconscious process to work. We always want to be consciously changing something – despite all the evidence that when we played at our best or learned at our fastest, we were less consciously involved in the doing. It was just happening. Think about it.

Comfort Zones

There is an interesting description of mental states used in skiing. Comfort, stretch and panic zones. Comfort zones are where boredom eventually sets in – we think our skill is greater than the challenge. Panic is where there is so much interference that it can paralyse us – we think the challenge is so much greater than our skill that it has become a threat. Stretch is where most improvement takes place – the challenge is in proportion to our skill.

When we play well, don't we go back to the clubhouse and say 'I don't know how it happened but it just clicked today. I didn't think about it, I just did it'? Our integrator and executor are doing a great job of learning and performing for us. When we play badly, we are often busy thinking about what we are doing and trying to change things. We don't want to trust our subconscious to take control, or, as Timothy Gallwey describes it, 'trust and let go'. The idea of allowing our subconscious to do things for us can become a threat and produce the effects that we have discussed before, yet we need to learn to use it.

Most of what we experience is actually processed subconsciously. The trick is to manage the conscious portion of our experience so that it points the subconscious in the right direction. My hope is that we now have some understanding of how our brain drives our body. If this has seemed incomplete in any way, that's because our understanding of this field is. We have advanced a long way and yet we are still in our infancy in psychology compared with swing technique.

So now let's turn our attention to some ways of applying these theories practically to our golf. Once more, the principle is that our brain drives our body, and our perception drives our brain. When we manage what we perceive by managing the stimuli, then we have our best chance of reaching peak performance.

Summary

- Mental skills allow us to perform our physical skills.
- Understanding something doesn't mean that we can do it.
- People have an innate ability to learn.
- Experiencing what we are doing helps us learn and perform.
- Managing our perception is the key to experiencing.
- Interference blocks our perception of the world.
- We can harness this ability to learn by understanding brain dominance and sensory modes.

THE WAY FORWARD

Now that we have explored some of the basics about how we generate performance, we can begin to apply some of the theory practically. To help us perform at our peak, our brains need a map to follow – just as a computer needs a programme to follow. The key elements of this map are:

- It enables us to identify the direction we want to go in, i.e. goal-setting;
- It is structured in such a way that we are able to recognise when we reach our goal, using language that our brain understands;
- It provides us with a plan of specifically what we will do (the tools or exercises) and how we will do it (practice), and gives us a means of recognising or rewarding ourselves for doing things that produce the desired results.

So, first let's talk about goal setting.

GOAL SETTING

Goals are what give our brains a direction to go in. Most of us use them to one degree or another in our lives, career development or hobbies. We have often heard about successful people having very clear objectives. But just saying 'I want to get better at golf' or 'I want to win a tournament', as many people do, doesn't give your brain much to go on. It is like saying 'I want to travel' to our travel agent. He would need to know where we want to go and how we want to get there, to be able to help. So do our brains!

SELF ASSESSMENT GRID

On the left list the skills and qualities that you believe are essential to your becoming a better golfer. Score yourself from 1 to 10 against each item. 10 means you are as strong as you think you can be on that particular item, 1 means that you think you are very weak on that particular item.

If you are interested in a more neutral opinion of your skills, you might ask other people who know you and your skills to fill out a column for you.

SKILL QUALITIES	OTHER	OTHER	OTHER	AV.	SELF
Long Game	8	8	7	7.7	6
Fitness	4	5	3	4	4
Short Game	6	7	7	6.7	8
Practice	2	3	4	3	6
Mental Skills	7	6	6	6.3	5
Grip	9	10	9	9.3	9

REMEMBER THIS IS NOT THE TRUTH !

WHERE AM I RIGHT NOW?

To help us set useful goals we need to know where we are starting from – where we are right now. Imagine trying to get to London from Glasgow. We have a map that shows us where London is but does not show Glasgow. It makes it very hard to know what the next step should be to get to London.

In the grid opposite you will see an exercise I use to help golfers think through the current status of their golf so that they have a better idea where they are starting from. I ask people to think of the skills and qualities that are essential to become a good golfer and list them down the left column (driving, bunker play, physical fitness, concentration etc.). Then I ask them to rate themselves from 1 to 10 on each item where 1 means that they are very weak on that item, and 10 means that they are as strong as they think they could be. I also invite them to ask other people who are familiar with their game and whose opinions they trust to fill in a rating for them, and then take the average of those scores.

We then look at the two sets of data. One is the self-score that they gave. This often shows up gaps in their awareness – they say 'I did not realise it until I thought about it …'. The other is a way of injecting some neutral opinion into their thinking as a check on the accuracy of their own assessment. When there is a gap of 2 or more (plus or minus) between the self-score and the other score, it warrants some extra attention as to why.

Both of these pieces of data point to where some change might be useful and setting goals is the first step in this change process.

The three aspects of goal setting are:
• Making the goals SMART;
• The difference between learning and performance goals;
• Putting the goals into the language of our brain.

SMART GOALS

We can and will talk about goals in several different ways, but in each of these ways, to make them useful we need to make them SMART. This stands for:

Specific
Measurable
Achievable
Relevant
Time-phased

Yes, But …

In teaching most pros have run into the 'yes but' syndrome. In a beginner, it manifests itself when the student says that he wants to be a better golfer. The pro works with them for half an hour and at the end of that time they can hit the ball up in the air. Significant progress! The pro asks 'How are we doing?' The student replies 'Yes it's OK, but it doesn't go very far, does it?' So the pro works for another half hour with the student and the ball goes much further.

'How are we doing now?'
'Yes it's going further, but it's not very straight, is it …?'
And so it goes on. No matter what happens, the student always says 'Yes but …' because his goals were not set accurately at the outset.

Specific Goals need to be specific so that we can easily identify what they are and where they will lead us. When we say 'I want to be a better golfer', it is so vague that no matter what we do we can (and usually do) say to ourselves. 'Yes I am improving but I'm still not good enough'. In other words, we aren't yet perfect. We need to specify how we will recognise that we are a better golfer. Here are a few examples:

1 'I want to eliminate my slice. In practice, I want to be able to drive 5 out of 10 balls into an imaginary fairway without slicing, and 3 out of 10 when I am on the golf course.'
2 'I want to be able to hit 9 out of 10 shots with a full body turn.'

Measurable This is so that we know when we have attained them. Unless we can measure our performance against the goal we are aiming for, we will never know whether we have attained it which means we never get to feel successful. So, building on the second example above:

1 'I want to be able to hit 9 out of 10 shots with a full body turn which to me means getting my hips and shoulders rotated another quarter-turn.'

Now we have something tangible to measure, so that we can recognise any change in our turn using video and expert observation.

Achievable Our goals need to be achievable (and challenging) so that they don't become boring or threatening. We have to believe that the goal is achievable or it creates interference for us. As Csikszentmihayli and Loehr found out, if we think that the goal or challenge is too difficult for our level of skill, it will be threatening to us and produce worry, anxiety, tense muscles and poor performance, (see diagram opposite) e.g.

1 'In practice, I want to be able to drive 5 out of 10 balls without slicing and 3 out of 10 when I am on the golf course. I have only been been able to hit 1 shot in 10 without slicing so far.'

This implies a 500% improvement ...

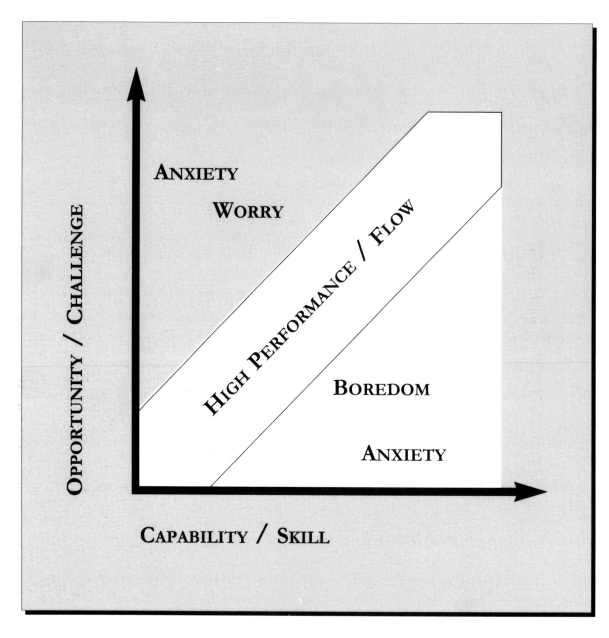

2 'I want to be able to hit 9 out of 10 shots with a full body turn. I have never done it so far.'

An infinite percentage improvement!

If we believe the goal doesn't challenge our level of skill then it will produce boredom and eventually anxiety, low energy levels and loss of focus, (see diagram above) e.g.

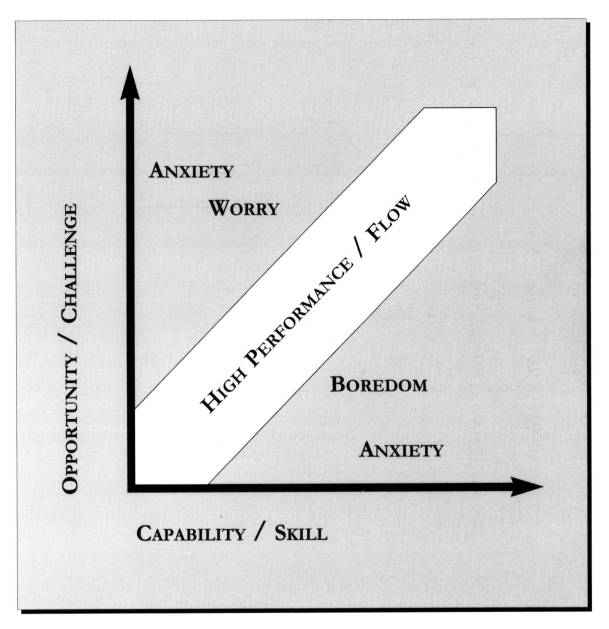

1 'In practice, I want to be able to drive 5 out of 10 balls without slicing and 3 out of 10 when I am on the golf course. I can do 4 out of 10 in practice already.'

2 'I want to be able to hit 9 out of 10 shots with a full body turn. I can do 8 out of 10 already.'

There is not much challenge in either case, so neither of these goals generates much enthusiasm or energy.

When we think our goal is achievable but that we will have to stretch for it, then we are more likely to get a quiet mind, relaxed muscles, and focused attention – the flow state, (see diagram on page 81) e.g.

1 'In practice, I want to be able to drive 5 out of 10 balls without slicing and 3 out of 10 when I am on the golf course. Currently I think I can do 3 on the range and 2 on the course.'

2 'I want to be able to hit 9 out of 10 shots with a full body turn. I can do 6 at the moment.'

A 66% improvement in both examples. Challenging but not impossible!

Relevant When a goal is not meaningful to us then it becomes hard to muster the energy necessary to go after it. Goals imposed by other people, or those which we adopt because we have seen other people be successful with them, usually don't have enough relevance to excite us, e.g.

1 'I want to be able to hit 9 out of 10 shots with a full body turn. I can do 6 at the moment but I'd rather try to improve my length off the tee.'

2 'I want to but not all that much' is what's being said here. The goal is not relevant to me right now.

Time-phased When do we want to achieve the goal by? The time-phase that we set will be an important factor in determining how achievable and relevant the goal is to us, e.g.

1 'In practice, I want to be able to drive 5 out of 10 balls without slicing and 3 out of 10 when I am on the golf course by the end of this half-hour practice session. Currently I think I can do 3 on the range and 2 on the course.'

The time-phase might make this unrealistic or not achievable.

2 'I want to be able to hit 9 out of 10 shots with a full body turn by the end of the month. I can do 6 at the moment and I practise 3 times a week.'

Now we are getting the goal to be **SMART**.
We sometimes hear people talk of short, medium and long-term

Intensive practice. The Noel Hunt Golf Show

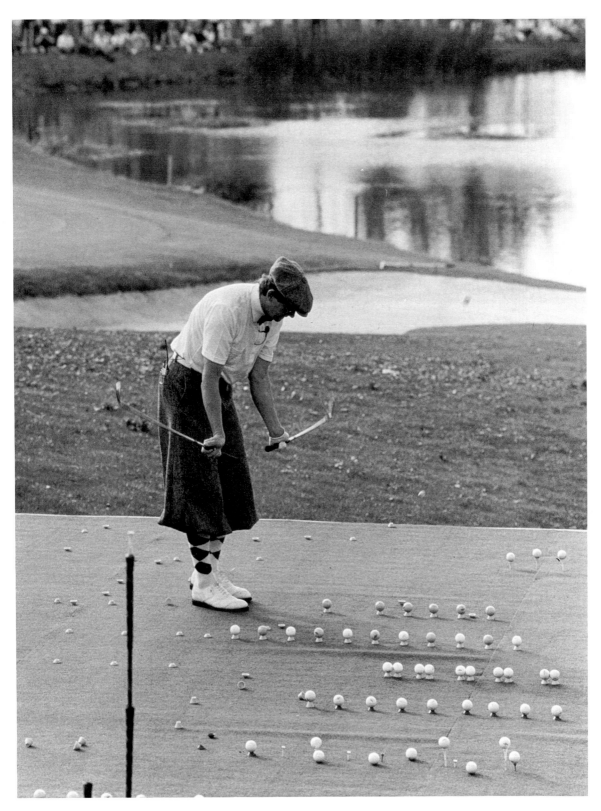

Was that SMART Alan?

Making the goal SMART helped me stop the 'yes buts' when playing the first hole at Whitchurch a few years ago. The lady pro I was playing with asked me what I wanted to achieve at this hole. I said 'Merely get the ball onto the green.' It was a par 3 and about a 5-iron for me. The pro went first and topped the ball into the rough. Now I was really nervous! I placed my ball on the tee, reminded myself that the goal was to just get on the green and swung. I watched as the ball arched straight at the flag. It stopped about ten yards short. I turned to my partner who was congratulating me on my shot, and said 'Yes but if only I had taken a 4-iron I would have been inches from the hole!' She turned to me and said 'What was your goal?' 'Yes but ...'. She interrupted 'What did you say your goal was?' She reminded me of my smart goal so that I could measure my success and feel more confident about the next shot instead of less confident because I hadn't done it perfectly!

goals. It can be useful to use all of them in golf, as long as they are made SMART.

Short-term goals extend from right now to, say, three months away. We set them in terms of a goal for our practice session today (holing 60% of 6 foot putts), or a goal for some specific improvement by the end of that three-month period – or both. It means deciding specifically what we want to walk away from our practice session having achieved. If we have made them SMART, short-term goals allow us to experience some immediate progress and that helps to boost our energy level – so crucial for performance – and our confidence. If we give some careful thought to our practice session goals we can experience a success every time we go out. And there is nothing like success to breed further success. The little wins that we accumulate in the short-term add up, and over a period of time they all contribute to the long-term 'big win' and all help us develop the habit of being successful – the performance loop again.

Medium-term goals go from three months to two years. They give us significant check points en route to our final destination. If our long-term goal is a handicap of 5, then a medium-term goal might be to get down to single figures within twelve months.

Long-term goals are anything that goes beyond two years. They are a way of expressing our vision or dreams more tangibly. They keep us inspired and energised to take action. The youngster wants to become a pro, the club golfer wants to break 80, etc.

LEARNING AND PERFORMANCE GOALS

Making any goal SMART makes a difference to how useful the goal can be. However, there are other facets of setting goals worth considering.

PERFORMANCE GOALS

Many of us understand the importance of setting goals for ourselves and when we set them, most of us tend to set performance goals such as winning the monthly medal by June, or shooting below 90 within one year, or finishing in the top ten in a tour event by July. All of these are examples of performance goals, but while they are important and necessary to us, there is one problem they each have in common. They can all be affected by forces outside our control, e.g. other players, or the weather.

Imagine our goal is winning the monthly medal by June. We play our best golf ever, walk in with a nett 65, and deserve to win and would have won any other medal that year. But someone else is also having a good patch, and as a result has scored a nett 64. Any other time we would have achieved our goal, but now we walk away feeling dissatisfied because it seems as if we have failed. It's the same if we aim for a top ten finish. In fact, we have watched tour players seemingly do all they needed to do to make the Ryder Cup team only to be pipped at the last minute by someone winning a big money tournament just before selection. They may do very little else all season but if our goal was to be in the Ryder Cup team, then again we have failed. If we aim to break 90, the week we are on our best form may have the worst weather of the season. Yet again we have failed.

To make performance goals as effective as possible, we need to find ways of measuring the change in our performance that are less dependent on external factors. Let's look at an example. Think of a tournament golfer new to the tour. He wants to win his first tournament. Whether the event is large or small does not matter – he just wants to get a win under his belt. He has come close to winning several times and is now beginning to lose heart. All he can perceive now is failure.

Our first step is to identify how he could measure his performance improvement other than by winning. He decides that his playing statistics might be a useful guide. At the moment he can hit, on average, 12 greens in regulation and his putting average is 31 per round. Together we set goals for the next three months of increasing the average number of greens hit in regulation to 14, and lowering his putting average to 30. These goals are independent of any other player's performance. The weather may still play a part, but that's life.

If our goal is to win the monthly medal or reduce our handicap by 6 strokes by the end of the year we similarly need to identify specifically what we need to do in order to have our best chance of winning. It may mean only two 3 putts per round, it may mean not risking cutting of the dog leg at the 8th or laying up on the long 12th instead of trying to reach the green in two.

Although performance goals are vital, we need to be careful in how we use them – make them as specific and independent of other people as possible.

"

Watch for big problems; they disguise big opportunities.

"

H. Jackson Brown Jr

LEARNING GOALS

Whatever is going on in terms of our performance, there is always something we can be learning. Let's go back to how we perceive and interpret events and consider two extremes.

If we land our ball in a bunker we are very likely to interpret this as a disaster and get into all the dilemmas of trying too hard to recover. There is another way to interpret what has happened. We could see this as an opportunity to learn how to be better at getting out of bunkers. We may not have achieved our short-term goal of getting on to the green in two, but we could use the new circumstances to help us fulfil our medium-term goal of being better at bunker play.

Learning goals can be used in any circumstances – even the most adverse. The pro who is watching his score climb above 80 as he reaches the 17th tee can either blow out completely or use it as a time to learn and practise composure. It is also an opportunity to learn and practise keeping his energy level high even under pressure.

Welshman Phillip Price had a very successful first year on the European Tour in 1991. However, when he turned professional a lot of people thought that he wasn't good enough to survive on the tour. We had been working together for a couple of years and at the beginning of the season we set learning goals under several headings. One was to use a couple of focusing exercises that he had found particularly helpful (they are described in Chapter Five) as often as he could. Together we established a learning goal of using the exercise on every putt (instead of about half the putts). Another learning goal was not to allow himself to look to the crowd as if he was in trouble (more of this later also). Both of these goals were irrespective of the score. He was to do them as a means of improving his golf with a view to helping his score in the medium- and long-term.

Phillip found that he played his best when he was busy with improving his game (his learning goals) rather than when he was concerned with his score (his performance). He pursued his learning goals and played better golf as a result.

When shown these paragraphs for approval, Phillip commented 'There was also another important learning goal for me. In the last year I've also learned how to be with players like Ian Woosnam and not be frightened. In the past I would go out to play feeling very nervous if I was drawn to play with a person of that stature. But I realised that if I was going to improve as a player I had to learn how to handle these situations. I decided that I would just notice

Price and Woosnam. World Cup 91

Ian Baker-Finch, 1991 British
Open – the winning experience

what I was sensing as I played. I intended to get used to being with and playing with players of that stature. I knew I needed to if I am going to continue to grow as a player.' Another example of a learning goal.

If we have clear, explicit learning goals we can have a success every time we go out and that is what increases our confidence. And the more we learn, the faster our performance improves.

GOALS AND THE LANGUAGE OF OUR BRAIN

Our goals have the most effect on us when we set them in the language that our brain understands, i.e. in terms of what we see, feel and hear. If we win a tournament that's great, but it is what we see, hear and feel as we win that influence us and drive our behaviour.

A common example of this is when we are thinking of buying a car. Just thinking of the word car will not have much effect on us. It's the things that come into our mind when we think about a car that have an effect on us. Some of us will see what the car will look like, we may spend time looking at brochures. To a significant degree we will base our decision to buy on how the car looks to us and how we think we will look driving it. Others of us will think about how we will feel when we drive it, or when other people look at it. And others will want a particular kind of engine noise to listen to. The word car has a different meaning to each of us.

Winning also has a different meaning to each of us. At the extreme, some of us think about what we will hear people say about us. Others think about what we will feel like walking up the 18th fairway or going into the clubhouse. And others will see an applauding crowd at the end of the day. Most of us think about our goal in some combination of these modes.

So, if our goal is to be a better golfer, we first need to define how we will recognise that we are better, i.e. make the goal SMART. Then we should decide what we will see, hear and feel when we reach that SMART goal. Using our previous example:

'I want to be able to hit 9 out of 10 shots with a full body turn by the end of the month. I can do 6 at the moment and I practise 3 times a week.'

We can add to this what we think we will see, hear and feel when we achieve the goal. For instance we might **see** a different shape to the flight of the ball or a lower score on our card. We might **feel** more relaxed in our arms or more energy at the end of a round or a practice session. We might **hear** a crisper sound as we strike the ball or people telling us how much our swing has changed.

If we identify what we will be seeing, hearing and feeling when we achieve our goals, we bring those goals to life, and that makes it much easier for our brains to recognise that we are progressing and helps our subconscious take us in that direction.

REVIEWING GOALS

An essential part of making goals useful for us is to review them at regular intervals. This tells us how far along the road towards our goal we are, and whether we are even on the right road. Whenever the 'due' date for a short-term goal comes up, we need to review it to check our progress, and reset the date if necessary. With medium- and long-term goals we need to review them at regular intervals and not wait for the due date before checking and/or resetting them.

'OWN GOALS'

There are a couple of very common pitfalls or misuse of goals that I bump into time and time again.

SELF-INFLICTED WOUNDS

Some of us have a very strong tendency to beat ourselves up emotionally if we don't reach our goals. We judge ourselves very harshly and use what we call 'the failure' as an excuse for all kinds of responses that simply do not help. These responses, ranging from self-criticism that causes us to lose confidence, to anger (the club-throwers and spectator-blamers), are usually a way of saying to the world 'I normally play much better than this. I am angry so that you will know I can play better'. It results in us getting very little pleasure from the game.

POTATOES

Here is an analogy that I borrow from Stephen R. Covey, a management guru whose thinking about what makes people effective I have found very helpful. He is illustrating two extremes in terms of how we tackle goal setting.

Imagine we were trying to grow potatoes (or a new golf swing). We want to give the seeds the best chance of survival so we plant them in fertile soil one day. What many of us do is dig them up again the next day, to check on how the roots are doing. We do the same thing day after day and so the roots are never able to take hold. At the other extreme, are those of us who never dig them up to check on progress. We never know whether they have any disease or are growing correctly until it is too late.

Let's think about how this manifests itself in golf. In the first approach we are constantly evaluating ourselves against our goals after every shot. We judge our success or failure too soon, and never giving our concentration time to deepen. We recognise these golfers by the amount of self-criticism they give themselves. They are frequently to be heard saying 'yes but' or 'if only' to themselves. They are often frustrated with their progress and sometimes even angry with themselves.

In the second approach, we don't check where we are against our goals often enough and the result is that we can be way off course before we even know it. We recognise these golfers by the way they are still working on fixing their swing five years into their golf game. (I don't mean refining, I mean fixing!) They are likely to continue working on an area of their game long past the point where it is helpful. They never know when to stop because they never check on their progress

Goals should be used as road signs along the way. They tell us the direction we want to go in and how we will know when we get there. They also tell us the direction we are actually heading in and how far towards that point we have progressed. And that is all. How far we have gone towards them is rarely an indication of our potential to play the game of golf.

Summary

- Goals should be SMART – specific, measurable, achievable, relevant and time-phased.

- We should use both performance and learning goals.

- Goals are more powerful when described in sensory terms.

MANAGING THE STIMULI

Now that we have a clearer idea of where we want to go, it is time to increase our experience of what is happening right now so that our subconscious can do its job of making the appropriate corrections for us. We can do that by managing the stimuli that we interpret which then generate our reaction.

Think of it as if our brain works like a video recorder. When the record button is pushed all sights and sounds that we experience are recorded on the video tape. When the tape is played back we get a high quality image and sound. Imagine if, when the record button is pushed, we were also able to push down the play button at the same time. Not only would we record the sights and sounds coming from outside the camera (the external stimuli) but we would also record again the previous sights and sounds. When we came to play back the 'master' tape, the quality of the new recording would be awful.

That is what the learning process is like for a lot of us. What we perceive is so distorted and jumbled by our beliefs, assumptions and fears, that the resulting recording that we try to play back is jumbled and distorted. What we 'see' and therefore act upon is not an accurate representation of reality. And as we said before, garbage in = garbage out.

What this means to us is that the more we can ensure the input into our brains is quality input, the more chance we have of getting quality output. And we do that by managing the stimuli that come into our performance loop.

FOCUSING ATTENTION – QUIETENING THE MIND

I had always thought of concentration or focused attention as something we either had or didn't have. It was in our genes. One

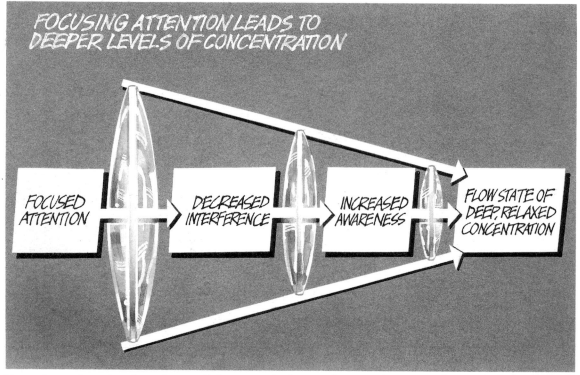

FOCUSING ATTENTION LEADS TO
DEEPER LEVELS OF CONCENTRATION

FOCUSED
ATTENTION → DECREASED
INTERFERENCE → INCREASED
AWARENESS → FLOW STATE OF
DEEP, RELAXED
CONCENTRATION

Focused attention – how it works

of the most important lessons for me as I searched for ways to raise performance was that focusing attention is a trainable skill.

In focusing our attention several things happen at the same time. We manage the stimuli that are coming in to our performance loop so that what gets through triggers the right reaction. As we do this, the interference that is sometimes present in our mind is reduced because we cannot pay attention to the internal stimuli and the external stimuli at the same time. Our awareness of what we are doing increases, and the quality of what we are experiencing, i.e. the stimuli entering our brain, is higher so our learning rate speeds up and/or our level of performance of the skills that we already have increases.

One of the easiest ways to help ourselves focus our attention is to harness something that we are all born with – curiosity. If we think about it, we all have it. When we walk down the street and see someone pointing up to the roof of a building we always look up to see what they are so interested in. As human beings our curiosity can be almost insatiable.

The essence of a focusing exercise in golf is to ask ourselves to notice some detail about what we are doing. In order to notice that thing, we have to focus even more of our attention on it. The simplest example of this kind of exercise I have seen was devised by Timothy Gallwey.

BACK-HIT (the bounce-hit of golf)

The back-hit exercise devised by Timothy Gallwey

The back-hit exercise, to me, is a focusing exercise that has the highest probability of making the most difference to the greatest number of people. What I ask people to do is this:

'At the moment your club gets to the top or the limit of your backswings say "back" out loud. When your club meets the ball (i.e. the moment of impact) say "hit" out loud. Don't worry about where the ball goes or how you hit it.'

Most people when they first attempt to do this will say the words 'back' and 'hit' after the actual events – they say 'back' when their club is already moving forwards and 'hit' after the ball has already left their clubface. In many cases they don't say 'hit' until the ball has travelled about 30 yards!

The dialogue usually continues in this way:

'Did you say "back" when the club got to the top of the backswing and "hit" when it met the ball?'

'Yes, I think so.'

'That's interesting, because to me it sounded as if you said both the "back" and the "hit" after those events occurred.'

'Really?'

'Well, let's try it again. Go back and check whether or not that was actually the case.'

As they hit the next few balls they are busy noticing whether or not they say the 'back' and 'hit' on time (i.e. as those events actually happen). Now their attention on what they are doing increases.

'Yes, you are right!'
'Put some more attention on saying the "back" and "hit" and less on the other things you are trying to think about. Do you see the ball when the club strikes it?'
'No.'
'Then how do you know when to say hit?'

Now they realise that they don't have their full attention on the exercise.

'Find out what you are looking at if it isn't the ball.'

As they try to notice what they see, their attention focuses much more specifically on their visual sense and what they actually 'see'. As a result they are much less caught up in trying to swing correctly, avoiding trouble etc. Their minds become calm and quiet, the interference goes down, their experience of what is actually happening goes up and their performance improves (see Chapter 2). They are no longer trying to do something that they think they cannot do (hit a good shot) which is threatening for them. Instead they are now trying to do something they think they can do (just notice where their attention is). This reduces the threat, helps produce the 'flow' state and allows the subconscious to do its work.

Sometimes when people do this exercise the pitch and tone of their voices changes dramatically. In fact when they say 'back-hit' on their practice swing they will use a very even relaxed tone of voice. When they say it as they hit the ball it comes out very loud and strangled because some of their attention is still caught up on other things. I then suggest that they say back and hit in the same way as when they practise swing.

Now their attention is caught up with something they can control – their voice – rather than something they can't control – their swing. And again they will hit the ball better. Of course, it will not work this way for everyone but it can help nine out of ten players when they are not playing well.

As a focusing exercise this can and indeed has been used on any shot from the driver to the putter, and by any level of player from beginner to professional. What is hard to believe or trust is that by getting our attention focused, the subconscious will make the necessary swing corrections that enable us to hit the ball better. Sometimes beginners can swing correctly without even understanding what they are doing differently. That's how powerful our brain is.

ALTERNATIVE FOCUSES

There is almost an infinite number of focuses that we can use to streamline our attention, and they all help us to manage the stimuli coming into our brains which can deepen our experience of what is happening right now – the present. The more accurate our experience of what our senses are telling us right now, the more learning takes place, and the more learning that takes place, the better our performance is. So here are some other ways we might get our attention focused. We can often classify them into sensory groupings.

VISUAL FOCUSES

The Ball This is not new but is often lost because it is so obvious. Noticing what our eyes are seeing as we swing the club helps keep the video recorder in 'record' mode and the play button switched off. We don't try to see anything in particular, we are merely passive observers; we simply notice what our eyes are registering.

Broad or Narrow Some people find it useful to narrow their attention down to some very specific small detail of their visual field such as the writing on the ball (the letters that make up the manufacturer's name) or the shape and arrangement of the dimples on the ball around the maker's logo. Others find it more helpful to have a broad focus. Here our attention would be taking in a broad view of what our eyes are registering rather than just a small part of it. We might see the ball and the grass surrounding it.

The Hole Watching the hole rather than the ball can be a useful exercise when putting.

When we throw a ball at a target our instinct is to look at the target – not the ball – and this can be effective in putting also. Looking at the hole as we putt can take our conscious thought away from the stroke itself and enable our subconscious to do what we have already programmed it to do.

Colour This might seem strange at first. I had asked the touring

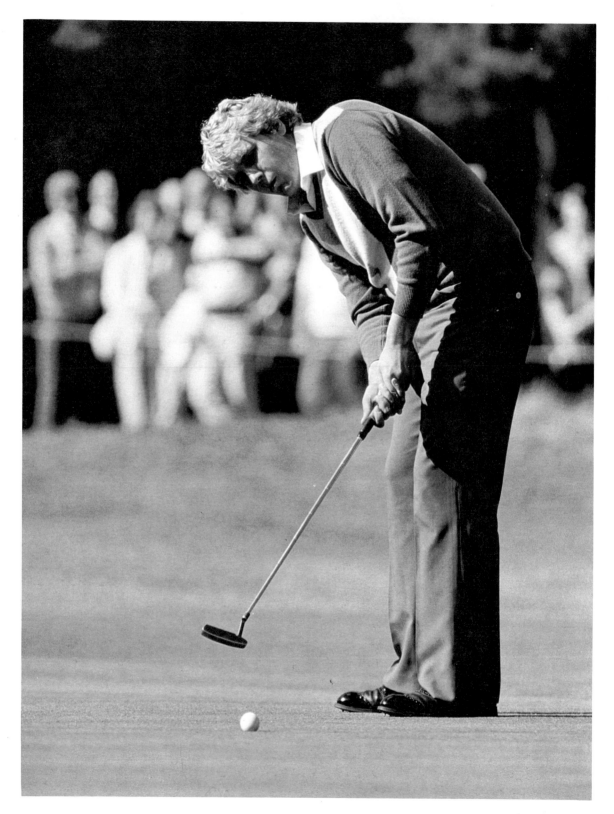

pro Richard Boxall 'What's it like when you play well?' I was looking for clues as to what triggered his peak performance state. His response was 'It's sort of blue.' I asked him what happened whenever he thought of the colour blue. He said that he felt more energised and enthusiastic, and less fearful. So I suggested that he thought about or saw the colour blue when he felt his game needed a lift. He successfully used this technique some years ago in the last tournament of the season, the Portuguese Open, when he had to hole his final putt on the final hole of the final round to save himself from a visit to the tour qualifying school.

KINAESTHETIC FOCUSES

Smiling Forcing ourselves to smile as we hit the ball has to be one of the most embarrassing exercises on the golf course. Had I not seen it work, I would never have believed it could. I was watching an 18-handicapper struggle desperately to hit the ball straight. He was trying so hard to hit the ball well that his face was grimacing. He hadn't been able to get into any exercise so far, so I thought that this called for drastic measures. I asked him to smile when he hit the ball. No matter how he hit it or where he hit it he was to keep a smile on his face for the duration of his swing. It was so ridiculous it worked! It changed the stimuli coming into the brain and so he reacted differently. His muscles relaxed – they had to for him to smile. But it wasn't just his facial muscles. It was his arms and chest and legs as well. Remember, if we are playing badly then we really have nothing to lose in trying this kind of exercise.

Breathing Out Exhaling as we move the club towards the ball (not as we take it away) encourages our muscles to relax and also reduces anxiety (that's where the expression 'take a deep breath and ...' comes from). It seems to be most useful if the exhalation lasts for the duration of the forward swing of the club. Trying to do this for the whole of our swing is difficult to say the least – it could be terminal if you have a very slow swing! Some people find it useful to make the breath very forceful, they blow it out. Others find it better to make it a soft breath. Experimenting will tell you what is for you.

Feeling Our Body 1 Paying attention to how our body feels can provide some really useful ways to focus our attention and increase our experience of what we are doing, particularly as golf is so much about feeling what we are doing or kinaesthetic awareness.

David Feherty again provides a useful example of how we can do this. Every so often David has felt he has had problems with

(opposite) Richard Boxall

On putting...

When your mind is so absorbed with the physical action of making the putting stroke [i.e. when the video recorder is in 'play' mode] it's unlikely that you will ever move the putter away from the ball smoothly. When this happened I would usually miss the putt. In order to overcome this I needed to divert my mind's attention away from the physical task of producing a stroke and focus instead on some other simple task, one which I could be sure of doing successfully while I played. So I decided that as I made my stroke I would try to read as many letters of the manufacturer's name printed on the ball as I could. The more letters I could read, the smoother I found my stroke became, and eventually the concentration that I applied to doing this overcame the anxiety I had previously felt about the putt itself. In other words, my mind was now so busy concentrating on reading the letters on the ball [the video recorder was in 'record' mode] that it couldn't possibly interfere with the execution of the stroke.

David Feherty

his putting and one of the ways in which we eliminated these problems is to increase his awareness of what his body is doing as he putts (this is not necessarily a conscious awareness). We wanted to make sure that his subconscious (i.e. his computer) was getting good quality input.

He would practise putts from different positions on the putting green and I would ask him:

'What part of your body are you most aware of as you hit the putt?'

A typical response would be 'My hands'. I would then push him a little further:

'Just notice your hands and be aware of what they are doing. Tell me what is it about your hands that grabs your attention.'
He might say 'It's a sensation in the first two fingers of my right hand'.
'Notice when that sensation begins and ends in your putting stroke.'

When we had done this for about five minutes on his hands, we would repeat the same process on his arms, legs, head, trunk etc. Our purpose was not to analyse consciously what he was doing wrong. It was to keep his mind quiet and focused so that the input to his subconscious was of much higher quality. It was to help him manage the stimuli coming into his system. In a sense we were re-calibrating his feel of the shot.

Of course, this process of focusing on the sensations in our body can be used on any shot in the game. It's important to realise that what we think the shot should feel like is not what we are worried about in this exercise. We can imagine what we want to feel like before we practise each shot (more about mental rehearsal soon) but here we are only trying to be more aware of what the sensations actually are.

Feeling Our Body 2 Putting with our eyes closed is another way to increase feel. Our visual sense is a great suppressor of feeling. When we lose one of our senses the others automatically sharpen up to compensate, and if we close our eyes as we putt we become much more aware of the other sensations in our body. We can extend this exercise into calibrating our feel for distance and direction as follows.

(opposite) David Feherty on winning!

David Feherty 'blind putting'

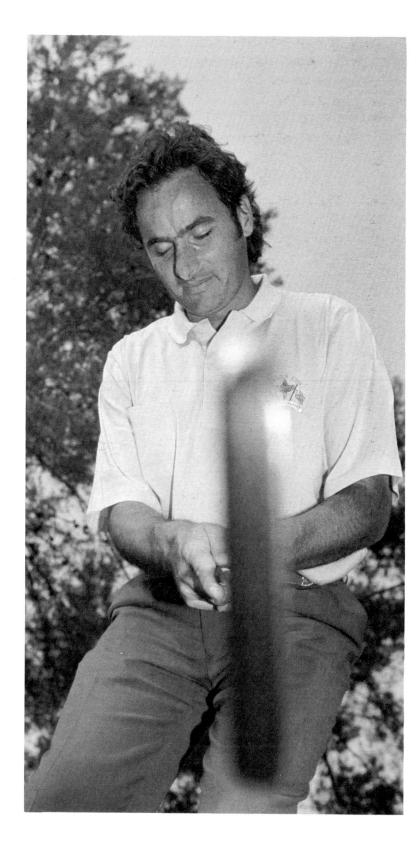

Aim at a hole. We then close our eyes and putt. With our eyes still closed we estimate how far long or short of the hole the ball has finished, and also how far left or right of the hole, all based on how the shot felt. Then we open our eyes and note how accurate our assessment was. The more we repeat this kind of exercise the better our 'feel' for these things becomes.

AUDITORY FOCUSES

Humming This is similar to the breathing out exercise. If we take a practice swing at the ball and at the same time hum one note, the sound will come out in an even pitch. If we try to do the same thing when we hit the ball the sound comes out with a lot more emphasis in the middle of it. If we make sure that our voice stays even as we swing through the ball we are likely to make a much smoother swing. To keep our voice even, we have to relax our muscles, and it can be easier to keep the sound of our voice even than to relax our muscles.

Impact Sound Every time the club meets the ball it makes a sound which is likely to be different on each shot. We can listen for how the sound varies from shot to shot. It may have a different pitch each time, it may be a long or a short sound, it may be loud or quiet. We may even hear the sound of the club moving through the air.

BETWEEN SHOTS

So far we have been talking about the things that we can focus on as we play each shot. But most of the time in golf is not spent playing shots. It is spent walking and waiting for our turn to play. It is therefore important for us to manage the stimuli or keep our minds quiet in these in-between periods.

We can do this in the same way that we did as we played the shots. Here are some examples of what we might focus our attention on as we walk or wait between shots. Always bear in mind that different focuses work for different people. You have to experiment to find out.

Visual The trees, crowd, colours of what we are looking at. The breadth or narrowness of our visual field – do we look down at our feet or do we have a broad view of the crowd or landscape. The shape of the next shot we want to play.

Kinaesthetic How does our body feel when we are walking? Are there particular sensations that stand out? Is our walk smooth or jerky, flexible or tight, relaxed or tense, balanced or unbalanced? Do we feel the right side more than the left, which part of us is warmest, how strong are any of these sensations? What does our breathing feel like?

Auditory What does our breath sound like? What other noises can we hear – the wind, crowd noise, motors running? How loud is what we hear? Does it change its pitch, tone, rhythm, tempo, direction?

There are three useful questions to apply to each of these focuses to help us keep our attention. They are:

What do I notice? – What specifically is easiest for me to notice about what my senses are telling me right now? Is it something I see, feel or hear?

When or where do I notice it? – When in the duration of the swing or when between the shots do I notice it? Where in my body do I notice it?

How much of it do I notice? – What is the intensity of the thing that I have noticed? A lot, a little, a medium amount?

These apply both as we are playing a shot or between shots. Trying to answer these questions forces us to pay more attention to the object of our attention, i.e. it focuses our attention.

IMAGINATION

Our imagination has an extraordinarily powerful effect on our performance. It can be both positive or negative, depending on what we are imagining. When we experience interference it is usually our imagination at work. We try to anticipate what the future will be, and often imagine the worst. We found out with the pendulum experiment in Chapter 1 that whatever is in our mind is reflected physically in some way – however small. Mental rehearsal and imagery techniques harness this principle in a positive way and are used by many leading athletes (and business people). They can be very powerful if we let ourselves get fully into them.

Phillip Price, using his
imagination by acting as if . . .

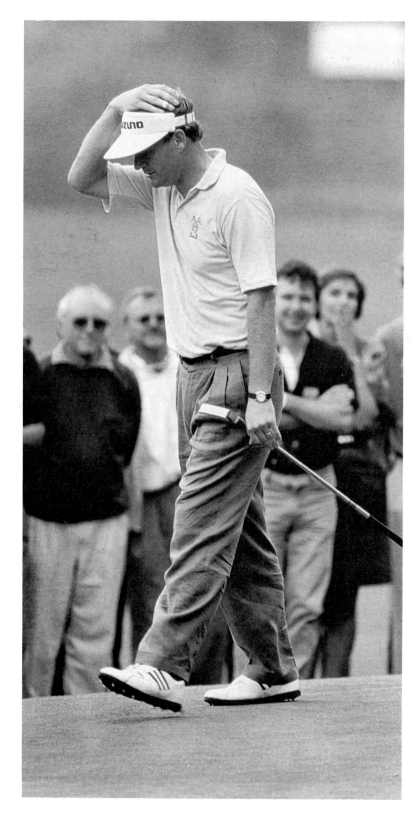

Sandy Lyle. Sometimes you can't
act as if ...

IMAGERY

Acting as if ...

1 Think about what your posture is like when you play well. Compare it with what it is like when you play badly. Most people hang their head and slouch when they aren't on top of their game. It is a reflection or representation of what is happening in their mind – their mental state. We can prevent ourselves becoming like this or change things when we are like this, by maintaining our 'winning' posture no matter how we are playing or acting as if we were winning. We walk with our head up at the same pace and rhythm as if we were playing really well. We hold the club the same way, we breathe the same way, we do everything exactly the same way as when we are playing well no matter what the result. Keeping his attention on the feel of his 'winning' posture was one way that Phillip Price kept his composure in his first season as a professional.

2 Secondly, we could think of a quality or attitude that we would like to exhibit as we play. For example we might want to swing more smoothly, or play with a more positive attitude. What we do is act as if we had this quality or attitude. It is as if we are acting the whole thing out before a movie camera. We need to exaggerate or ham up what we are doing for the camera. The key is to get so engrossed in the role play that it becomes real. The more we get into the acting, the closer our mental state gets to the one that we want – and our actions will follow on.

3 When we are putting we could imagine that the hole is the size of a dustbin. Putting into a hole of this size reduces the threat that we perceive and allows our muscles to relax. We only have to be 'in' the exercise for the few seconds of making the putt.

4 On any shot, short or long, we could imagine that we are 30 pounds heavier, as if we would sink into the ground and can feel our weight pressing down onto our ankles. Or we can imagine we are 30 pounds lighter so that we are so light we can barely feel the ground beneath us, and if there was a wind we would blow away. The aim, as always, is to get our attention focused. Although the object of focus may seem irrelevant it works well for some golfers.

5 We pretend that our club has a brain and talent all of its own – that it is the most well trained, experienced and capable club in the

Visualising – useful mental rehearsal

world. It knows what to do and how to swing, all we have to do is let it show us how. We do nothing but allow the club to show us what 'it wants to do'!

So far all of these focusing exercises have been things that we can do while we are actually playing our golf. However, there are also things we can do before we even get out on the golf course that can make a significant difference to the way we play.

MENTAL REHEARSAL

Every time we visualise a movement in our mind, it causes tiny little impulses to travel down our nerves into the relevant muscles and produces the movement in miniature. Each time an impulse travels down to a muscle, it makes it very slightly easier for the next impulse to travel down the same route between our brain and our body. It is as if a groove is being cut (some people refer to it as building muscle memory). The more we image something over and over in our mind, the easier it becomes to do that thing.

Here is a way to go about mentally rehearsing our golf. Sit in a chair or lie on the floor and get comfortable and breathe normally. Keep your hands and feet uncrossed and close your eyes. Get as

The One That Got Away

We often get back to the clubhouse and tell everyone about the shot we dumped into the water at the 15th. If what we think about over and over is reflected in our actions, what are we rehearsing for the next time we play that hole?

relaxed as possible (when you do this you change the brain wave to a slower frequency that is much more conducive for learning).

Each time you exhale, mentally count from 10 to 1, one number on each exhalation. Form an image in your mind of whatever it is you want to do, perform or learn and experience yourself doing it. In your mind's eye see, hear and feel it in as much detail as possible as if it is happening to you right now. Allow yourself to enjoy the exercise and get into the experience as much as you can. If it's a swing, play it over and over in your mind. If it's an attitude, imagine what you would see/hear/feel if you had that attitude.

When you feel ready (give it at least a few minutes) mentally count on each exhalation from 1 to 10. As you get to 10 open your eyes and come back to the room you are sitting in.

Like all techniques, some of us will find mental rehearsal easier than others, but like most skills, it gets easier with practice.

I've Done It Before

When David Hemery won the gold medal for the 400 metres hurdles in the 1968 Olympic Games in Mexico, I asked him 'Did it feel strange when you were out there running the final?' 'No,' he replied. 'In my mind I had rehearsed that race many times. I knew every step I was going to take and so it was easy.'

Summary

- Our ability to focus attention can be developed.

- Focusing our attention is a way to manage the stimuli entering our performance loop.

- We can focus our attention by noticing or being interested in some detail of what we are doing right now.

- Focused attention is as important between shots as during them.

- Our imagination is a very powerful tool that can be used in a constructive way.

Basketball

A classic piece of research was carried out with basketball players. They were divided into three groups. One did no practice at free throws (where the player stands in front of the group and throws the ball into the hoop). The second did ordinary physical practice, throwing balls into the hoop. The third did only mental rehearsal. The first group made no improvement, the second significant improvement and the third made the same improvement as the second group. Those doing only mental rehearsal improved as much as those doing the physical practice.

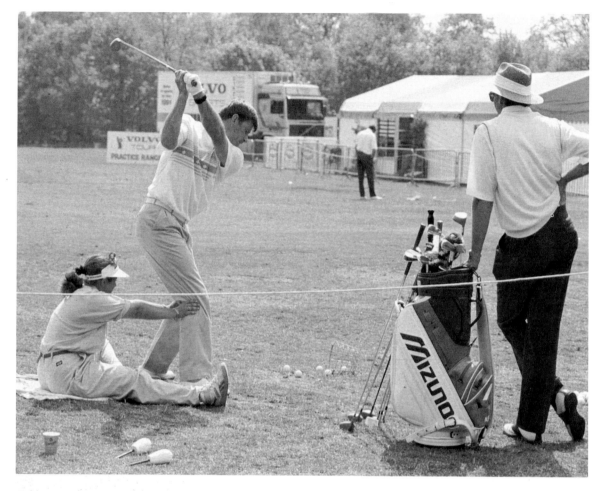

Faldo, Leadbetter and Fanny
Sunesson. Practice making
perfect?

PRACTICE MAKES PERMANENT

'Practice makes perfect.' What a great saying. It is not true, but it is a great saying. Hasn't that been drummed into us throughout our lives?

'No one ever became a great player without practice.' Now that I can agree with. But there are hundreds of professional golfers – and thousands of amateurs – who have been out on the practice ground until their hands have blistered and they have never improved their score. Why is this? Because we have only got part of the story.

Practice makes permanent. I'll say it again, but louder!

Practice makes permanent.

Whatever we do over and over again becomes a habit. So, if we are not getting the improvement that we want in our game, then we are not repeating the appropriate behaviour. Here are three elements that I find useful when thinking about practice.

1 **Knowledge** what to do and why to do it
2 **Skill** mastery of what to do
3 **Desire** want or commitment to what to do

For our practice to be effective we need to know what we should be practising, and why we should practise it. If we don't understand why we are practising, then it can make it very hard to generate the high energy that we need for 'high performing' or quality practice. We develop the skill through repetition of the components of that skill in low pressure situations. From that comes our results.

Knowledge and desire together with practice build skills. Skill and practice together produce results. Results reinforce our desire and thirst for knowledge.

LOBOTOMIES

At the beginning of this book we said that it is not possible to separate the mental from the physical without a lobotomy. No mental state means no physical activity. Comatose! So anytime that we practise we are making both the physical and the mental parts of our game habitual.

For instance, when we shake our head after each shot and then try harder to get our swing right the next time, we ingrain the habit of trying harder as well as improving the swing. Therefore, we should not be surprised when we do the same thing when we get out on the course.

Much of the practice that I see is of marginal value to the golfers because it lacks organisation. I have worked with several tour pros who complained of problems with their putting and/or short game. As we investigated the causes, we discovered that they hardly practised this part of their game. It wasn't surprising that they weren't putting well; they hardly ever set foot on the practice putting green. Organising our practice in terms of accurate knowledge of what to do, and how to do it, can make a huge difference to how productive it is for us. So let's explore some ideas about how to and what to practise.

GOAL SETTING IN PRACTICE

As always, the first step in improvement is to decide which direction we want to go in and how to recognise it when we get there. With some careful thought we can set SMART goals not only for each practice session, but also to encompass the different parts of a practice session. Why so much detail? Because every time we achieve a goal it sends a message to our subconscious that we are succeeding and this is what builds our self-confidence (or removes our self-doubt). There are some examples in Chapter 4 on goal setting that will show you how we might go about doing this.

The majority of golfers that I meet know what they want to achieve but have not addressed a fundamental decision they need to make: are they willing to pay the price to achieve that goal? To achieve anything worthwhile takes effort. It can be fun and reward-ing but at the same time it does take sustained effort. Most amateurs and a lot of pros look for quick fixes which are usually much more difficult to sustain.

Think for a moment about what we would do if we wanted

to increase the strength in our right arm. We would lift small weights on a regular basis until the muscles in our arms adapt. When we first start training it feels very uncomfortable and a voice in the back of our mind tries to tell us that we can put off the training until tomorrow, or maybe that we can do without it altogether. We continue because we know that if we do, we will grow stronger. This is how it is with all skills. We have to be willing to pay the price – whatever that may be – if we want to achieve our goals. During the years it took Nick Faldo to remodel his swing with David Leadbetter his results were so poor that people questioned whether or not he had made the right decision.

The price we have to pay is usually one or other or both of the following:

- an investment of time to build or refresh our skills (amateurs particularly often don't even get out on the practice ground);
- a change in behaviour that will feel unfamiliar and even uncomfortable for some people.

Most of us are resistant to change. We prefer to remain and feel more comfortable with the familiar and the known, even if it is not producing the result we want. (Better the devil we know than the devil we don't know.) Yet implicit in improvement is change and doing things differently. If we are not willing to pay the price, then let's decide that at the outset and change our expectations of what we want out of our golf.

By the way, if you learnt to walk and talk, you have the ability to learn to play this game. You may not play in the Open but you can certainly have fun. And if at the moment you are not improving and not enjoying your golf, you are either practising the wrong things or aren't willing to pay the price.

PLAYING GOLF VS BUILDING A SWING

Most of the practice that I see golfers of all levels do goes like this. They stand on the range with about 100 balls and hit them one after the other with a few practice swings in between. It is a great way to learn to swing the club correctly (given some of the caveats we have explored in this book). But then they become puzzled when they find it hard to sustain what they did in practice when they are out on the course playing golf. It's often because they have failed to understand the difference between developing the skills –

I believe the brain is like a muscle – like any other it can be improved.

Tennis superstar Ivan Lendl

Smarter, Not Harder

There are several touring pros who have cut down the amount they practise to 100 balls a day. This was as a result of discovering that the quality of their attention was poor after that many balls. They became bored and their practice became counter-productive. Of course the price they had to pay was the discomfort of everyone telling them that they would never improve if they didn't work harder. They decided it was more useful to work smarter.

what is often called the 'muscle memory' – and implementing the skills in the competitive environment – playing golf. They are different and demand different forms of practice.

BUILDING A SWING

If we are interested in building a swing or effecting some change in our swing we need to get the maximum number of repetitions with the highest intensity of experiencing those repetitons. We want to 'burn' the movement into our brain. Hitting lots of balls is invaluable provided that we can do it with the minimum of self-criticism and evaluation. The more we just notice what is happening, the faster things will change.

Lots of short practice sessions are much more useful than fewer lengthy ones. Pausing after every ten or so shots doesn't overload our attention span. One hour's quality practice four days a week is much more useful than four hours' practice once a week.

PLAYING GOLF

Beating balls as a means of practising our swing is useful but it isn't golf. In fact when we spend a lot of time practising this way, we are forming a habit we will never use on the golf course, i.e. hitting one shot after the other from the same spot with the same club. When we play the game we do the opposite. We play each shot from a different location, with a different club and we have on average 2.5 minutes between each shot. This means we need to become skilled at bringing our concentration together every 2.5 minutes. There is no way we will sustain peak concentration for the 4+ hours it takes to play 18 holes.

As far as practising in a way that is valuable in terms of improving our performance out on the course, we need to create a more realistic set of circumstances, and practise what we will be doing when we get out on the course. Once our swing is built to some degree, we could practise using a different club for each shot, with at least a one-minute interval between each swing. Playing from a different location each time is usually problematic, but we can at least aim at different targets on each shot and try different shapes on each shot as if we were playing a hole.

We can take this a stage further, and imagine that we are playing our home course. For example, if the first hole is a par-4, and we normally take a 3-wood from the tee, we pick our target and hit the 3-wood. We watch the flight of the ball and try to imagine where it would have come to rest if we had actually been playing the first hole. Then, on the basis of how well we hit our 'tee-shot', we could plan our second shot that we would have left to the green. If we hit a good 3-wood, then our next shot might be with a 9-iron, so we take our 9-iron, and imagine playing the ball right down the flag. If we pushed our 3-wood, we might decide that we need to manufacture a cut-shot around a tree in order to get onto the green, and so we try to conjure up a left-to-right shot and so on. In theory we could play a full 18 holes like this, and in doing so we would be practising the focusing and imaging skills that we have been discussing in previous chapters.

In putting we could place four balls in a circle, each ball being 6 inches from the hole. We putt them all. Assuming we sink them all, we replace them at 1-foot intervals around the hole and do the same again. We keep repeating the process placing the balls at ever greater distances until we miss one. At this point we go back to the beginning and start the process all over again. Let's say that we missed the 15th putt. Imagine what it will be like when we get to the 15th putt on the next series of putts. The pressure gets much closer to that experienced in competitive play. And that's what we are trying to practise.

What we practise becomes a habit. That's why it is important to make at least a part of our practice as close to the real thing as we can.

RIGHT BRAIN IT

We discussed right and left brain theory earlier in the book. I want to remind you at this stage that our practice time can be used to build our skill at whichever side of our brain needs developing. The left-brainers could be practising and getting used to letting go and thinking less about their shot as they swing. The right-brainers could be going through a thorough pre-shot routine and practising working out their yardage.

DIARIES

Many touring pros keep a diary of what they do on the golf course and what happens inside them as they play each round – particularly in respect of what they see, hear and feel as they play and what the result of what they saw, heard and felt was. Then, when I meet up with them we look back over a few weeks of note-taking and search

Pressure

I believe that the ability to withstand pressure comes with experience. It's a learning process, but it is possible to manipulate your mind to such a degree that you forget about the circumstances. Difficult though it is [when you are under pressure], you try to clear your mind of the fact that a shot or a putt is important.

On the 18th green at Kiawah, I just followed my usual routine. I studied the line and once I had a clear picture in my mind of the ball heading along that line to the hole I committed myself totally to the putt and concentrated on the speed. Even if it turns out to be a bad read, it's always better to pick a definite line and stick to it. You make a much better stroke when you do that. The importance of developing and then adhering to a pre-shot routine cannot be over-stated. You should develop your own style — not just on the green, but for all shots — and then stick to it. And all the time that I'm surveying a putt, my concentration and awareness are increasing.

Bernhard Langer

for any trends. It is one of the ways in which we discover what the cause of a problem shot is: sometimes it's just the lack of practice time given to that shot, other times it might be what their dominant way of approaching the game is – right- or left-brained and/or dominant sensory mode. Keeping a diary is a useful way of keeping ourselves on track.

WHEN WRONG IS RIGHT

When we practise, most of us are obsessed with swinging the club in the 'correct' way – whatever our version of that is – and quite rightly so. But there are times when practising the wrong thing is actually doing the right thing. For example, imagine we are trying to increase our awareness or feel on our short pitches. It can be helpful to experiment and execute it in all kinds of 'wrong' ways such as a stance that is too open to the target line, or a clubface

The Langer limbo – withstands the pressure. Ryder Cup 87!

that is too open or closed to the ball. We may never want to execute the shot this way when we play, but doing so in practice increases our experience base. We feel new sensations and our awareness of what we can do with our body and the club increases. In essence we are exaggerating the shot to expand our range of awareness. We don't spend all of our practice time doing this, just enough to have fun with it.

REWARD SYSTEMS

All good coaches and managers know that the most effective way to make any behaviour a habit is to reward the behaviour each time it happens. So when we swing the club the way the pro wants us to, he or she will praise us. Each time we do something the pro likes we get a reward – our ego gets stroked. We like the 'payoff' of the compliment and so we seek to get more of them by repeating

Reward the Right Behaviour

While on holiday, the 10-year-old son of a friend of mine idly put his hand into the coin return slot of a public telephone and found a coin. The rest of the holiday was spent searching every public telephone he saw to see if there were any coins left behind. His behaviour had been rewarded and was subsequently repeated – and how.

the same behaviour. We expect others, especially coaches, to 'reward' us in some way when we do something well.

We can harness this effect by setting up reward systems for ourselves, without waiting for the coach or anyone else to do it for us. We tell our subconscious that it did a great job for us by giving ourselves something we want when we achieve a specific goal. It needs to be something that we would not do in the normal course of events so that it stands out as a reward.

Here is an example from a tour pro:

Goal	Reward
Complete my learning goals for the week	6 new music cassettes
Finish in the top thirty	12 new music cassettes
Finish in the top ten	New stereo system
Win the tournament	New Porsche

Now of course the rewards for us would look a lot different from these (well, most of us anyway). And it does not have to be expensive or even cost anything. However, it does need to be something that we recognise we would not ordinarily have done for ourselves.

Many of us fend off the potential reward. How often have you heard someone dismiss a compliment by saying 'Oh it was nothing', or 'I was lucky, I don't normally hit my driver that straight'. We also say to ourselves 'I don't need to reward myself specifically. I know when I have done well'.

We can set up reward systems for our practice as well as our competitive play. Completing the goals for a week's practice may deserve the book we wanted to buy or a beer with our friends. We do, however, need to be careful. Used inappropriately, encouragement or rewards can also cause us to move into the trying too hard mode. We can become too attached to pleasing our coach, or getting the 'present' and as a consequence get over anxious about the results.

COMMITMENT

Commitment is like concentration in that we all use the word, we all think we know what we mean and we all find it very hard to do. Yet nothing happens without it. Unless we are committed to our plan of action then we are not going to stay with it and nothing will change.

Most of the high performers I have encountered – both in

Nick Faldo, one of the most committed golfers in the world

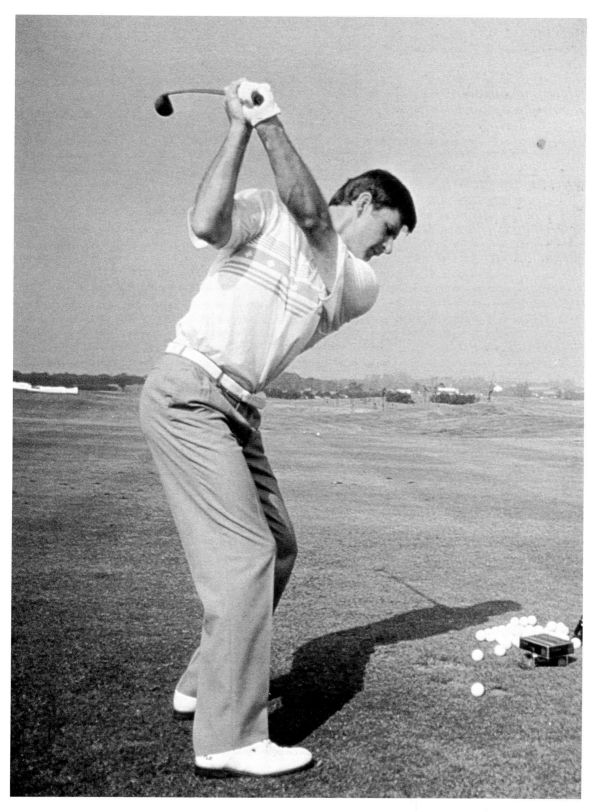

“

Whatever you can do or dream you can do, begin it. Boldness has genius, power and magic in it. Begin it now.

”

Goethe

Severiano Ballesteros, so committed he'll do his own repairs

sports and in business – attribute a high proportion of their success to their level of commitment to what they are doing. Commitment in golf is generated in the same way as anything else – by a strong desire for the game, or some aspect of it.

We become committed when we are very clear about our purpose in playing golf. By purpose I mean the reason why we play – the payoff for us. By the way, even for the top golfers the payoff is usually more to do with pride of performance than money. Even though the financial payoff is sometimes huge, it is the pursuit of excellence that most of them are after.

The less clear we are about whether we really want to be playing in this tournament today, or spend an afternoon on the practice ground or even go out at all, the more difficult it is for us to put our energy into what we are doing. Commitment starts with a vision of our innermost desire, a dream, an admission of our innermost wants, and it builds as we translate it into action.

Successful people usually have a vision that fires them up so much it becomes an irresistible force. We've all heard about or know people who display a tremendous commitment to doing something that really matters to them. I know of several young golfers who are happy to make an eight-hour journey so that they can get 90 minutes' tuition with their favourite coach. Their commitment to their vision of being great golfers is total. Others spend hours working on their putting on the practice green while their friends go out for a game on the course. They are prepared to make sacrifices to do something that fits in with their vision – to be a better golfer. If we want to improve, we must demonstrate a similar degree of commitment.

Bill Marré, a very good friend of mine, and I were discussing commitment in the business world, and I described to him how I sometimes test a golfer's commitment. He suggested that one way to think about commitment is to ask ourselves. 'What if I had to do that thing? What if not doing it wasn't an option?' As I asked myself those questions I began to realise that it forced me to consider possibilities that I had been avoiding.

Let's look at a real example. Several years ago I was working with David Feherty, who for some reason was quitting on his shots in the downswing. He couldn't seem to commit himself to release the clubhead freely through the ball. On the practice ground he was fine, but when playing in a tournament he would quit a fraction of a second before impact, with the result that he would push the ball out to the right. Each time we would meet, he would say that he

really meant to commit to the shot, but that he didn't seem to be able to 'stay with it' when the pressure was on.

So I asked him 'If I threatened to blow your brains out if you quit on any shot, would you stay committed?'

His response was immediate. 'Absolutely. I would make more money doing that than winning this week. And I wouldn't even have to make the cut.'

Then I altered my approach slightly and asked him 'If I promised you £50,000 if you commit fully on each shot irrespective of where the ball went, would you take it?'

Again the reply was 'Absolutely.'

'So committing is within your control if you absolutely had to do it?'

'Yes, I suppose it is' he said.

'OK David, how much money can you afford to lose?'

He started to say £1000 (things were different in those days) and then smelt a rat.

'Five hundred pounds!'

'Here's an idea. Given that you have said that if you had to you would commit on every single shot, how about writing a cheque to your favourite charity for £1000 and leaving it with me. If you commit on every shot in the next week I will return it you. If I think for whatever reason that you quit even on one shot I will send the cheque off. Of course your money would not be in any danger because you have said this is within your conscious control if the stakes are high enough (the stakes being loads of money or getting your head blown off). It will only be in danger if you don't mean to do what it takes to commit.'

Now of course he was faced with the prospect of quitting and losing money, never mind not earning any by missing the cut. He would be much better off committing.

I then added: 'David, only say yes to this if you are sure you can do it. Once you sign the cheque the deal is on and only negotiable with my agreement.'

If this sounds harsh to you, it was. But David and I had worked together for some time and there was a high level of trust between us. And the choice to do it was entirely his. He thought this was a painful but useful exercise to try out and duly wrote a cheque for £1000 to the RSPCA. He also called me a few unrepeatable names as he left.

When I met David again one week later I was talking to the new Italian Open champion. He had finally understood what

Until one is committed, there is hesitancy, the chance to draw back, always ineffectiveness, concerning all acts of initiative (and creation). There is one elementary truth, the ignorance of which kills countless ideas and splendid plans: that the moment when one definitely commits oneself, then providence moves too. All sorts of things occur to help one that would never have otherwise occurred. A whole stream of events issues from the decision, raising in one's favour all manner of unforeseen incidents and meetings and material assistance which no man could have dreamt would have come his way.

From *The Scottish Himalayan Expedition* by W. H. Murray

(opposite) Commitment – Woosnam style!

123

commitment really meant to him. And he told me to send the cheque off anyway!

Nothing happens without our commitment to see it through to the end.

Summary

- Practice makes permanent.

- Knowledge and desire are important factors in practice.

- Practise:
    With clear goals;
    A little and often;
    What you will do when you play;
    Both sides of our brain;
    The wrong way sometimes.

- Use a diary to stay on track.

- Reward yourself when you succeed.

- Commit!

THE LAST WORD

It has been 20 years that I have been involved in the vocation and business of helping people improve their performance in all kinds of activities. This book is not an attempt to capture it all, it is a collection of some things that golfers have found useful in their pursuit of peak performance.

I am frequently asked what I think are the most common reasons why people don't perform to their potential. My answer at the time of writing this book is this:

1 We don't act on what we already know. We don't do anything with the knowledge and skill we already have in our possession.
2 We are not willing to pay the price in order to realise our objectives – in particular we are unwilling to take a risk and make a mistake and learn from that mistake.
3 We are reluctant to be ruthlessly objective about whether what we do actually produces the result we want. We labour under false beliefs.
4 We don't organise ourselves properly.
   To me the most effective solutions are the simple ones. As my American friend would say (the one with the telephone-addict son!) 'this does not have to be rocket science'.

This book was born from my experiences with the golfers and others who have sought my help with their games, and who had the patience and the trust in me to endure my experiments with performance enhancement. Some of them became 'casualties'. They didn't 'survive' the experiments. Sorry folks, but I'm still learning too. Some of the survivors have been mentioned in this book.

My hope is that this book will enable you to make some sense of what is possible for your own performance, and help you find some ways to make some more steps in whatever direction you would like to go in.

Happy golfing.

If you would like further information on the material in this book, please write to:

InsideOut Development Ltd,
PO Box 2323,
London W8 62E

PICTURE CREDITS

Black and white

Allsport (David Cannon) 10, 16 (right), 17, 19, 38, 43, 83, 98, 105, 122, 116–117, (Simon Bruty) 11, (Michael Hobbs) 15, (Stephen Munday) 23, 102, 119, (Russell Cheyne) 39, (Rusty Jarrett) 49;

Peter Dazeley 16 (left), 36–37, 110, 121;

Keith Hailey 20, 88–89, 100, 106;

Phil Inglis 28;

Phil Sheldon 52–53, 87.

Colour Section

Allsport (Simon Bruty) 70 (above), (Steve Munday) 70 (below left);

Colorsport 66 (above), 67 (right), 68–69;

Peter Dazeley 65 (above), 66 (below), 67 (left), 72;

Mark Newcombe 70 (below right), 71;

Phil Sheldon (Jan Traylen) 65 (below).

INDEX

Page numbers in italic *denote illustrations*